Math

Placement Test
Secrets Study Guide

DEAR FUTURE EXAM SUCCESS STORY

First of all, **THANK YOU** for purchasing Mometrix study materials!

Second, congratulations! You are one of the few determined test-takers who are committed to doing whatever it takes to excel on your exam. **You have come to the right place.** We developed these study materials with one goal in mind: to deliver you the information you need in a format that's concise and easy to use.

In addition to optimizing your guide for the content of the test, we've outlined our recommended steps for breaking down the preparation process into small, attainable goals so you can make sure you stay on track.

We've also analyzed the entire test-taking process, identifying the most common pitfalls and showing how you can overcome them and be ready for any curveball the test throws you.

Standardized testing is one of the biggest obstacles on your road to success, which only increases the importance of doing well in the high-pressure, high-stakes environment of test day. Your results on this test could have a significant impact on your future, and this guide provides the information and practical advice to help you achieve your full potential on test day.

Your success is our success

We would love to hear from you! If you would like to share the story of your exam success or if you have any questions or comments in regard to our products, please contact us at **800-673-8175** or **support@mometrix.com**.

Thanks again for your business and we wish you continued success!

Sincerely,
The Mometrix Test Preparation Team

TABLE OF CONTENTS

Introduction

Thank you for purchasing this resource! You have made the choice to prepare yourself for a test that could have a huge impact on your future, and this guide is designed to help you be fully ready for test day. Obviously, it's important to have a solid understanding of the test material, but you also need to be prepared for the unique environment and stressors of the test, so that you can perform to the best of your abilities.

For this purpose, the first section that appears in this guide is the **Secret Keys**. We've devoted countless hours to meticulously researching what works and what doesn't, and we've boiled down our findings to the five most impactful steps you can take to improve your performance on the test. We start at the beginning with study planning and move through the preparation process, all the way to the testing strategies that will help you get the most out of what you know when you're finally sitting in front of the test.

We recommend that you start preparing for your test as far in advance as possible. However, if you've bought this guide as a last-minute study resource and only have a few days before your test, we recommend that you skip over the first two Secret Keys since they address a long-term study plan.

If you struggle with **test anxiety**, we strongly encourage you to check out our recommendations for how you can overcome it. Test anxiety is a formidable foe, but it can be beaten, and we want to make sure you have the tools you need to defeat it.

1

Secret Key #1 – Plan Big, Study Small

There's a lot riding on your performance. If you want to ace this test, you're going to need to keep your skills sharp and the material fresh in your mind. You need a plan that lets you review everything you need to know while still fitting in your schedule. We'll break this strategy down into three categories.

Information Organization

Start with the information you already have: the official test outline. From this, you can make a complete list of all the concepts you need to cover before the test. Organize these concepts into groups that can be studied together, and create a list of any related vocabulary you need to learn so you can brush up on any difficult terms. You'll want to keep this vocabulary list handy once you actually start studying since you may need to add to it along the way.

Time Management

Once you have your set of study concepts, decide how to spread them out over the time you have left before the test. Break your study plan into small, clear goals so you have a manageable task for each day and know exactly what you're doing. Then just focus on one small step at a time. When you manage your time this way, you don't need to spend hours at a time studying. Studying a small block of content for a short period each day helps you retain information better and avoid stressing over how much you have left to do. You can relax knowing that you have a plan to cover everything in time. In order for this strategy to be effective though, you have to start studying early and stick to your schedule. Avoid the exhaustion and futility that comes from last-minute cramming!

Study Environment

The environment you study in has a big impact on your learning. Studying in a coffee shop, while probably more enjoyable, is not likely to be as fruitful as studying in a quiet room. It's important to keep distractions to a minimum. You're only planning to study for a short block of time, so make the most of it. Don't pause to check your phone or get up to find a snack. It's also important to **avoid multitasking**. Research has consistently shown that multitasking will make your studying dramatically less effective. Your study area should also be comfortable and well-lit so you don't have the distraction of straining your eyes or sitting on an uncomfortable chair.

 The time of day you study is also important. You want to be rested and alert. Don't wait until just before bedtime. Study when you'll be most likely to comprehend and remember. Even better, if you know what time of day your test will be, set that time aside for study. That way your brain will be used to working on that subject at that specific time and you'll have a better chance of recalling information.

Finally, it can be helpful to team up with others who are studying for the same test. Your actual studying should be done in as isolated an environment as possible, but the work of organizing the information and setting up the study plan can be divided up. In between study sessions, you can discuss with your teammates the concepts that you're all studying and quiz each other on the details. Just be sure that your teammates are as serious about the test as you are. If you find that your study time is being replaced with social time, you might need to find a new team.

Secret Key #2 – Make Your Studying Count

You're devoting a lot of time and effort to preparing for this test, so you want to be absolutely certain it will pay off. This means doing more than just reading the content and hoping you can remember it on test day. It's important to make every minute of study count. There are two main areas you can focus on to make your studying count.

Retention

It doesn't matter how much time you study if you can't remember the material. You need to make sure you are retaining the concepts. To check your retention of the information you're learning, try recalling it at later times with minimal prompting. Try carrying around flashcards and glance at one or two from time to time or ask a friend who's also studying for the test to quiz you.

To enhance your retention, look for ways to put the information into practice so that you can apply it rather than simply recalling it. If you're using the information in practical ways, it will be much easier to remember. Similarly, it helps to solidify a concept in your mind if you're not only reading it to yourself but also explaining it to someone else. Ask a friend to let you teach them about a concept you're a little shaky on (or speak aloud to an imaginary audience if necessary). As you try to summarize, define, give examples, and answer your friend's questions, you'll understand the concepts better and they will stay with you longer. Finally, step back for a big picture view and ask yourself how each piece of information fits with the whole subject. When you link the different concepts together and see them working together as a whole, it's easier to remember the individual components.

Finally, practice showing your work on any multi-step problems, even if you're just studying. Writing out each step you take to solve a problem will help solidify the process in your mind, and you'll be more likely to remember it during the test.

Modality

Modality simply refers to the means or method by which you study. Choosing a study modality that fits your own individual learning style is crucial. No two people learn best in exactly the same way, so it's important to know your strengths and use them to your advantage.

For example, if you learn best by visualization, focus on visualizing a concept in your mind and draw an image or a diagram. Try color-coding your notes, illustrating them, or creating symbols that will trigger your mind to recall a learned concept. If you learn best by hearing or discussing information, find a study partner who learns the same way or read aloud to yourself. Think about how to put the information in your own words. Imagine that you are giving a lecture on the topic and record yourself so you can listen to it later.

For any learning style, flashcards can be helpful. Organize the information so you can take advantage of spare moments to review. Underline key words or phrases. Use different colors for different categories. Mnemonic devices (such as creating a short list in which every item starts with the same letter) can also help with retention. Find what works best for you and use it to store the information in your mind most effectively and easily.

Secret Key #3 – Practice the Right Way

Your success on test day depends not only on how many hours you put into preparing, but also on whether you prepared the right way. It's good to check along the way to see if your studying is paying off. One of the most effective ways to do this is by taking practice tests to evaluate your progress. Practice tests are useful because they show exactly where you need to improve. Every time you take a practice test, pay special attention to these three groups of questions:

- The questions you got wrong
- The questions you had to guess on, even if you guessed right
- The questions you found difficult or slow to work through

This will show you exactly what your weak areas are, and where you need to devote more study time. Ask yourself why each of these questions gave you trouble. Was it because you didn't understand the material? Was it because you didn't remember the vocabulary? Do you need more repetitions on this type of question to build speed and confidence? Dig into those questions and figure out how you can strengthen your weak areas as you go back to review the material.

 Additionally, many practice tests have a section explaining the answer choices. It can be tempting to read the explanation and think that you now have a good understanding of the concept. However, an explanation likely only covers part of the question's broader context. Even if the explanation makes perfect sense, **go back and investigate** every concept related to the question until you're positive you have a thorough understanding.

As you go along, keep in mind that the practice test is just that: practice. Memorizing these questions and answers will not be very helpful on the actual test because it is unlikely to have any of the same exact questions. If you only know the right answers to the sample questions, you won't be prepared for the real thing. **Study the concepts** until you understand them fully, and then you'll be able to answer any question that shows up on the test.

It's important to wait on the practice tests until you're ready. If you take a test on your first day of study, you may be overwhelmed by the amount of material covered and how much you need to learn. Work up to it gradually.

On test day, you'll need to be prepared for answering questions, managing your time, and using the test-taking strategies you've learned. It's a lot to balance, like a mental marathon that will have a big impact on your future. Like training for a marathon, you'll need to start slowly and work your way up. When test day arrives, you'll be ready.

Start with the strategies you've read in the first two Secret Keys—plan your course and study in the way that works best for you. If you have time, consider using multiple study resources to get different approaches to the same concepts. It can be helpful to see difficult concepts from more than one angle. Then find a good source for practice tests. Many times, the test website will suggest potential study resources or provide sample tests.

Practice Test Strategy

If you're able to find at least three practice tests, we recommend this strategy:

UNTIMED AND OPEN-BOOK PRACTICE

Take the first test with no time constraints and with your notes and study guide handy. Take your time and focus on applying the strategies you've learned.

TIMED AND OPEN-BOOK PRACTICE

Take the second practice test open-book as well, but set a timer and practice pacing yourself to finish in time.

TIMED AND CLOSED-BOOK PRACTICE

Take any other practice tests as if it were test day. Set a timer and put away your study materials. Sit at a table or desk in a quiet room, imagine yourself at the testing center, and answer questions as quickly and accurately as possible.

Keep repeating timed and closed-book tests on a regular basis until you run out of practice tests or it's time for the actual test. Your mind will be ready for the schedule and stress of test day, and you'll be able to focus on recalling the material you've learned.

Secret Key #4 – Pace Yourself

Once you're fully prepared for the material on the test, your biggest challenge on test day will be managing your time. Just knowing that the clock is ticking can make you panic even if you have plenty of time left. Work on pacing yourself so you can build confidence against the time constraints of the exam. Pacing is a difficult skill to master, especially in a high-pressure environment, so **practice is vital**.

Set time expectations for your pace based on how much time is available. For example, if a section has 60 questions and the time limit is 30 minutes, you know you have to average 30 seconds or less per question in order to answer them all. Although 30 seconds is the hard limit, set 25 seconds per question as your goal, so you reserve extra time to spend on harder questions. When you budget extra time for the harder questions, you no longer have any reason to stress when those questions take longer to answer.

Don't let this time expectation distract you from working through the test at a calm, steady pace, but keep it in mind so you don't spend too much time on any one question. Recognize that taking extra time on one question you don't understand may keep you from answering two that you do understand later in the test. If your time limit for a question is up and you're still not sure of the answer, mark it and move on, and come back to it later if the time and the test format allow. If the testing format doesn't allow you to return to earlier questions, just make an educated guess; then put it out of your mind and move on.

On the easier questions, be careful not to rush. It may seem wise to hurry through them so you have more time for the challenging ones, but it's not worth missing one if you know the concept and just didn't take the time to read the question fully. Work efficiently but make sure you understand the question and have looked at all of the answer choices, since more than one may seem right at first.

Even if you're paying attention to the time, you may find yourself a little behind at some point. You should speed up to get back on track, but do so wisely. Don't panic; just take a few seconds less on each question until you're caught up. Don't guess without thinking, but do look through the answer choices and eliminate any you know are wrong. If you can get down to two choices, it is often worthwhile to guess from those. Once you've chosen an answer, move on and don't dwell on any that you skipped or had to hurry through. If a question was taking too long, chances are it was one of the harder ones, so you weren't as likely to get it right anyway.

On the other hand, if you find yourself getting ahead of schedule, it may be beneficial to slow down a little. The more quickly you work, the more likely you are to make a careless mistake that will affect your score. You've budgeted time for each question, so don't be afraid to spend that time. Practice an efficient but careful pace to get the most out of the time you have.

Secret Key #5 – Have a Plan for Guessing

When you're taking the test, you may find yourself stuck on a question. Some of the answer choices seem better than others, but you don't see the one answer choice that is obviously correct. What do you do?

The scenario described above is very common, yet most test takers have not effectively prepared for it. Developing and practicing a plan for guessing may be one of the single most effective uses of your time as you get ready for the exam.

In developing your plan for guessing, there are three questions to address:

- When should you start the guessing process?
- How should you narrow down the choices?
- Which answer should you choose?

When to Start the Guessing Process

Unless your plan for guessing is to select C every time (which, despite its merits, is not what we recommend), you need to leave yourself enough time to apply your answer elimination strategies. Since you have a limited amount of time for each question, that means that if you're going to give yourself the best shot at guessing correctly, you have to decide quickly whether or not you will guess.

Of course, the best-case scenario is that you don't have to guess at all, so first, see if you can answer the question based on your knowledge of the subject and basic reasoning skills. Focus on the key words in the question and try to jog your memory of related topics. Give yourself a chance to bring the knowledge to mind, but once you realize that you don't have (or you can't access) the knowledge you need to answer the question, it's time to start the guessing process.

It's almost always better to start the guessing process too early than too late. It only takes a few seconds to remember something and answer the question from knowledge. Carefully eliminating wrong answer choices takes longer. Plus, going through the process of eliminating answer choices can actually help jog your memory.

Summary: Start the guessing process as soon as you decide that you can't answer the question based on your knowledge.

7

How to Narrow Down the Choices

The next chapter in this book (**Test-Taking Strategies**) includes a wide range of strategies for how to approach questions and how to look for answer choices to eliminate. You will definitely want to read those carefully, practice them, and figure out which ones work best for you. Here though, we're going to address a mindset rather than a particular strategy.

Your odds of guessing an answer correctly depend on how many options you are choosing from.

Number of options left	5	4	3	2	1
Odds of guessing correctly	20%	25%	33%	50%	100%

You can see from this chart just how valuable it is to be able to eliminate incorrect answers and make an educated guess, but there are two things that many test takers do that cause them to miss out on the benefits of guessing:

- Accidentally eliminating the correct answer
- Selecting an answer based on an impression

We'll look at the first one here, and the second one in the next section.

To avoid accidentally eliminating the correct answer, we recommend a thought exercise called **the $5 challenge**. In this challenge, you only eliminate an answer choice from contention if you are willing to bet $5 on it being wrong. Why $5? Five dollars is a small but not insignificant amount of money. It's an amount you could afford to lose but wouldn't want to throw away. And while losing

$5 once might not hurt too much, doing it twenty times will set you back $100. In the same way, each small decision you make—eliminating a choice here, guessing on a question there—won't by itself impact your score very much, but when you put them all together, they can make a big difference. By holding each answer choice elimination decision to a higher standard, you can reduce the risk of accidentally eliminating the correct answer.

The $5 challenge can also be applied in a positive sense: If you are willing to bet $5 that an answer choice *is* correct, go ahead and mark it as correct.

Summary: Only eliminate an answer choice if you are willing to bet $5 that it is wrong.

8

Which Answer to Choose

You're taking the test. You've run into a hard question and decided you'll have to guess. You've eliminated all the answer choices you're willing to bet $5 on. Now you have to pick an answer. Why do we even need to talk about this? Why can't you just pick whichever one you feel like when the time comes?

The answer to these questions is that if you don't come into the test with a plan, you'll rely on your impression to select an answer choice, and if you do that, you risk falling into a trap. The test writers know that everyone who takes their test will be guessing on some of the questions, so they intentionally write wrong answer choices to seem plausible. You still have to pick an answer though, and if the wrong answer choices are designed to look right, how can you ever be sure that you're not falling for their trap? The best solution we've found to this dilemma is to take the decision out of your hands entirely. Here is the process we recommend:

Once you've eliminated any choices that you are confident (willing to bet $5) are wrong, select the first remaining choice as your answer.

Whether you choose to select the first remaining choice, the second, or the last, the important thing is that you use some preselected standard. Using this approach guarantees that you will not be enticed into selecting an answer choice that looks right, because you are not basing your decision on how the answer choices look.

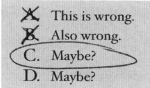

This is not meant to make you question your knowledge. Instead, it is to help you recognize the difference between your knowledge and your impressions. There's a huge difference between thinking an answer is right because of what you know, and thinking an answer is right because it looks or sounds like it should be right.

Summary: To ensure that your selection is appropriately random, make a predetermined selection from among all answer choices you have not eliminated.

Test-Taking Strategies

This section contains a list of test-taking strategies that you may find helpful as you work through the test. By taking what you know and applying logical thought, you can maximize your chances of answering any question correctly!

It is very important to realize that every question is different and every person is different: no single strategy will work on every question, and no single strategy will work for every person. That's why we've included all of them here, so you can try them out and determine which ones work best for different types of questions and which ones work best for you.

Question Strategies

⊘ READ CAREFULLY

Read the question and the answer choices carefully. Don't miss the question because you misread the terms. You have plenty of time to read each question thoroughly and make sure you understand what is being asked. Yet a happy medium must be attained, so don't waste too much time. You must read carefully and efficiently.

⊘ CONTEXTUAL CLUES

Look for contextual clues. If the question includes a word you are not familiar with, look at the immediate context for some indication of what the word might mean. Contextual clues can often give you all the information you need to decipher the meaning of an unfamiliar word. Even if you can't determine the meaning, you may be able to narrow down the possibilities enough to make a solid guess at the answer to the question.

⊘ PREFIXES

If you're having trouble with a word in the question or answer choices, try dissecting it. Take advantage of every clue that the word might include. Prefixes and suffixes can be a huge help. Usually, they allow you to determine a basic meaning. *Pre-* means before, *post-* means after, *pro-* is positive, *de-* is negative. From prefixes and suffixes, you can get an idea of the general meaning of the word and try to put it into context.

⊘ HEDGE WORDS

Watch out for critical hedge words, such as *likely, may, can, sometimes, often, almost, mostly, usually, generally, rarely,* and *sometimes.* Question writers insert these hedge phrases to cover every possibility. Often an answer choice will be wrong simply because it leaves no room for exception. Be on guard for answer choices that have definitive words such as *exactly* and *always.*

⊘ SWITCHBACK WORDS

Stay alert for *switchbacks.* These are the words and phrases frequently used to alert you to shifts in thought. The most common switchback words are *but, although,* and *however.* Others include *nevertheless, on the other hand, even though, while, in spite of, despite,* and *regardless of.* Switchback words are important to catch because they can change the direction of the question or an answer choice.

⊘ Face Value

When in doubt, use common sense. Accept the situation in the problem at face value. Don't read too much into it. These problems will not require you to make wild assumptions. If you have to go beyond creativity and warp time or space in order to have an answer choice fit the question, then you should move on and consider the other answer choices. These are normal problems rooted in reality. The applicable relationship or explanation may not be readily apparent, but it is there for you to figure out. Use your common sense to interpret anything that isn't clear.

Answer Choice Strategies

⊘ Answer Selection

The most thorough way to pick an answer choice is to identify and eliminate wrong answers until only one is left, then confirm it is the correct answer. Sometimes an answer choice may immediately seem right, but be careful. The test writers will usually put more than one reasonable answer choice on each question, so take a second to read all of them and make sure that the other choices are not equally obvious. As long as you have time left, it is better to read every answer choice than to pick the first one that looks right without checking the others.

⊘ Answer Choice Families

An answer choice family consists of two (in rare cases, three) answer choices that are very similar in construction and cannot all be true at the same time. If you see two answer choices that are direct opposites or parallels, one of them is usually the correct answer. For instance, if one answer choice says that quantity x increases and another either says that quantity x decreases (opposite) or says that quantity y increases (parallel), then those answer choices would fall into the same family. An answer choice that doesn't match the construction of the answer choice family is more likely to be incorrect. Most questions will not have answer choice families, but when they do appear, you should be prepared to recognize them.

⊘ Eliminate Answers

Eliminate answer choices as soon as you realize they are wrong, but make sure you consider all possibilities. If you are eliminating answer choices and realize that the last one you are left with is also wrong, don't panic. Start over and consider each choice again. There may be something you missed the first time that you will realize on the second pass.

⊘ Avoid Fact Traps

Don't be distracted by an answer choice that is factually true but doesn't answer the question. You are looking for the choice that answers the question. Stay focused on what the question is asking for so you don't accidentally pick an answer that is true but incorrect. Always go back to the question and make sure the answer choice you've selected actually answers the question and is not merely a true statement.

⊘ Extreme Statements

In general, you should avoid answers that put forth extreme actions as standard practice or proclaim controversial ideas as established fact. An answer choice that states the "process should be used in certain situations, if..." is much more likely to be correct than one that states the "process should be discontinued completely." The first is a calm rational statement and doesn't even make a definitive, uncompromising stance, using a hedge word *if* to provide wiggle room, whereas the second choice is far more extreme.

☑ BENCHMARK

As you read through the answer choices and you come across one that seems to answer the question well, mentally select that answer choice. This is not your final answer, but it's the one that will help you evaluate the other answer choices. The one that you selected is your benchmark or standard for judging each of the other answer choices. Every other answer choice must be compared to your benchmark. That choice is correct until proven otherwise by another answer choice beating it. If you find a better answer, then that one becomes your new benchmark. Once you've decided that no other choice answers the question as well as your benchmark, you have your final answer.

☑ PREDICT THE ANSWER

Before you even start looking at the answer choices, it is often best to try to predict the answer. When you come up with the answer on your own, it is easier to avoid distractions and traps because you will know exactly what to look for. The right answer choice is unlikely to be word-for-word what you came up with, but it should be a close match. Even if you are confident that you have the right answer, you should still take the time to read each option before moving on.

General Strategies

☑ TOUGH QUESTIONS

If you are stumped on a problem or it appears too hard or too difficult, don't waste time. Move on! Remember though, if you can quickly check for obviously incorrect answer choices, your chances of guessing correctly are greatly improved. Before you completely give up, at least try to knock out a couple of possible answers. Eliminate what you can and then guess at the remaining answer choices before moving on.

☑ CHECK YOUR WORK

Since you will probably not know every term listed and the answer to every question, it is important that you get credit for the ones that you do know. Don't miss any questions through careless mistakes. If at all possible, try to take a second to look back over your answer selection and make sure you've selected the correct answer choice and haven't made a costly careless mistake (such as marking an answer choice that you didn't mean to mark). This quick double check should more than pay for itself in caught mistakes for the time it costs.

☑ PACE YOURSELF

It's easy to be overwhelmed when you're looking at a page full of questions; your mind is confused and full of random thoughts, and the clock is ticking down faster than you would like. Calm down and maintain the pace that you have set for yourself. Especially as you get down to the last few minutes of the test, don't let the small numbers on the clock make you panic. As long as you are on track by monitoring your pace, you are guaranteed to have time for each question.

☑ DON'T RUSH

It is very easy to make errors when you are in a hurry. Maintaining a fast pace in answering questions is pointless if it makes you miss questions that you would have gotten right otherwise. Test writers like to include distracting information and wrong answers that seem right. Taking a little extra time to avoid careless mistakes can make all the difference in your test score. Find a pace that allows you to be confident in the answers that you select.

⊘ Keep Moving

Panicking will not help you pass the test, so do your best to stay calm and keep moving. Taking deep breaths and going through the answer elimination steps you practiced can help to break through a stress barrier and keep your pace.

Final Notes

The combination of a solid foundation of content knowledge and the confidence that comes from practicing your plan for applying that knowledge is the key to maximizing your performance on test day. As your foundation of content knowledge is built up and strengthened, you'll find that the strategies included in this chapter become more and more effective in helping you quickly sift through the distractions and traps of the test to isolate the correct answer.

Now that you're preparing to move forward into the test content chapters of this book, be sure to keep your goal in mind. As you read, think about how you will be able to apply this information on the test. If you've already seen sample questions for the test and you have an idea of the question format and style, try to come up with questions of your own that you can answer based on what you're reading. This will give you valuable practice applying your knowledge in the same ways you can expect to on test day.

Good luck and good studying!

14

Arithmetic

Computations with Integers and Fractions

This section measures your ability to correctly perform mathematical operations involving integers (positive and negative whole numbers and zero) and fractions (which may be either negative or positive.) The mathematical operations used in these problems include addition, subtraction, multiplication, and division. As a result, you must be comfortable performing these four operations when they involve negative and positive numbers.

Two positive integers can be added using simple rules of addition and will always yield a positive result. Add two negative integers together as if they were positive and then change the sign of the answer to negative. When one integer is positive and the other is negative, take the number with the smaller absolute value and subtract it from the larger. Next, change the sign of the answer to be the same as the sign of the number with the larger absolute value.

For example, to add 5 and −7, subtract 7 − 5 and then change the sign of the answer to a negative sign since 7 is greater than 5 and −7 is negative:
$$5 + (-7) = -2$$

Subtracting one integer from another can be solved by changing the problem to an addition problem and using the rules for addition. First, change the operator from subtraction to addition. Next, reverse the sign of the second integer. Last, add the integers together.

For example, to calculate −5 − 2, change it to addition and then follow the rules for addition:
$$-5 - 2 = -5 + (-2)$$
$$= -7$$

When multiplying or dividing two integers, perform the operation as if the numbers were both positive and then change the sign of the answer as follows: If the two integers have the same sign, then their product is positive; if they have different signs, then their product is negative. In addition to the rules above, special steps must be taken when dealing with fractions. One rule of fractions is that if you multiply or divide the numerator and denominator of a fraction by the same number, the result is an equivalent fraction (i.e. the fractions are equal to one another.)

For example, $\frac{1}{2}$ and $\frac{3}{6}$ are equivalent fractions because if you multiply the numerator and denominator of $\frac{1}{2}$ by 3, the result is $\frac{3}{6}$:
$$\frac{1}{2} \times \frac{3}{3} = \frac{3}{6}$$

When adding or subtracting fractions, first find a common denominator to both fractions. The best choice is a number called the lowest common denominator (LCD), which is the smallest number for which both denominators are factors. Once you find this value, rewrite each fraction as an equivalent fraction whose denominator is their LCD. Then add or subtract the numerators and put the answer over the LCD.

For instance, to add $-\frac{1}{6}$ and $\frac{5}{9}$, first rewrite them with the LCD of 6 and 9, which is 18:

$$-\frac{1}{6} \times \frac{3}{3} = -\frac{3}{18}$$
$$\frac{5}{9} \times \frac{2}{2} = \frac{10}{18}$$

Then add the numerators and put the result over 18.

$$-\frac{1}{6} + \frac{5}{9} = -\frac{3}{18} + \frac{10}{18}$$
$$= \frac{-3 + 10}{18}$$
$$= \frac{7}{18}$$

Similarly, to compare two fractions (i.e. determine which is greater) or put a list of fractions in order, rewrite them so that they have the same denominator and order them based on the numerators.

There are an infinite number of equivalent ways to write any fraction. The best choice is to express fractions in their lowest (or simplest) terms. A fraction is in lowest terms when its numerator and denominator do not have a common factor greater than 1. If a fraction is not in lowest terms, divide the numerator and denominator by their greatest common factor (GCF.) The GCF is the largest number that is a factor of both the numerator and denominator. For example, the fraction $\frac{4}{12}$ is not in lowest terms, because both 4 and 12 share a GCF of 4, and thus can be rewritten as $\frac{1}{3}$.

Multiplying fractions does not require finding a common denominator. Simply multiply the numerators together to create the new numerator, and multiply the denominators together to create the new denominator. It is a good practice to make sure that both fractions are first written in lowest terms, and factors common between the numerator of one fraction and the denominator of the other are cancelled out, to simplify the multiplication. Always express the final result in lowest terms.

Dividing two fractions is done by changing the problem to a multiplication problem and then using the rules for multiplication. First, change the operation to multiplication. Next, invert (or flip) the numerator and denominator of the second fraction.

For example, divide $\frac{2}{3}$ by $\frac{4}{5}$ as shown below. Note that $\frac{2}{3}$ and $\frac{5}{4}$ can be reduced prior to multiplication by cancelling out a factor of 2 in both the numerator and denominator:

$$\frac{2}{3} \div \frac{4}{5} = \frac{2}{3} \times \frac{5}{4}$$
$$= \frac{1}{3} \times \frac{5}{2}$$
$$= \frac{5}{6}$$

Some of the problems in this section involve more than one operation. Consequently, students must understand how to follow the order of operations to answer the questions correctly. A helpful mnemonic for the order of operations is "PEMDAS," which stands for "Parentheses, Exponents, Multiplication, Division, Addition, Subtraction." If a problem involves many different operations, first calculate the values inside parentheses, then compute the value of exponential expressions, then perform any multiplication, then division, and lastly addition and subtraction. Always remember to simplify fractions before working with them in expressions.

COMPUTATIONS WITH INTEGERS AND FRACTIONS QUESTIONS

1. $5(3-9) \div 3 =$
   a. -10
   b. 2
   c. 5
   d. 20

2. $\dfrac{4-(-12)}{-9+5} =$
   a. -8
   b. -4
   c. -2
   d. 4

3. $4\left(-\dfrac{1}{2}+\dfrac{3}{5}\right) =$
   a. $\dfrac{2}{5}$
   b. $\dfrac{4}{5}$
   c. 1
   d. $\dfrac{6}{5}$

4. Order $\dfrac{7}{15}, \dfrac{9}{20}, \dfrac{2}{5}$, and $\dfrac{13}{30}$ from least to greatest.
   a. $\dfrac{2}{5}, \dfrac{9}{20}, \dfrac{13}{30}, \dfrac{7}{15}$
   b. $\dfrac{2}{5}, \dfrac{13}{30}, \dfrac{9}{20}, \dfrac{7}{15}$
   c. $\dfrac{9}{20}, \dfrac{2}{5}, \dfrac{13}{30}, \dfrac{7}{15}$
   d. $\dfrac{13}{30}, \dfrac{2}{5}, \dfrac{9}{20}, \dfrac{7}{15}$

5. $\dfrac{3}{8} \div \dfrac{6}{11} =$
   a. $\dfrac{9}{44}$
   b. $\dfrac{15}{88}$
   c. $\dfrac{11}{16}$
   d. $\dfrac{33}{56}$

Computation with Decimal Numbers

This section measures your ability to correctly perform mathematical operation involving decimal numbers. Decimal numbers are numbers with at least one digit after the decimal point. The digits after the decimal point (called the number's decimal places) represent quantities less than one. The first place to the right of the decimal point is called the tenths place, the second place is called the hundredths place, the third is called the thousandths place, and so on. Any decimal can be quickly converted to a fraction (though a potentially unwieldy one) as in the example below:

$$5.8139 = 5 + \frac{8}{10} + \frac{1}{100} + \frac{3}{1000} + \frac{9}{10,000}$$
$$= \frac{58,139}{10,000}$$

The mathematical operations used in the problems in this section include addition, subtraction, multiplication, and division. As a result, students must be comfortable performing these four operations when they involve decimal numbers.

Add and subtract decimal numbers by first aligning the two numbers vertically, making sure that the decimal points are lined up one under the other. This will ensure that all corresponding decimal places (the tenths place, the hundredths place, etc.) are lined up as well. If one number has less decimal places than the other, add trailing zeroes until the number of decimal places are equal (3.2 is equal to 3.20.) Then add (or subtract) the corresponding decimal places starting from the right and working to the left, and bring down the decimal point at the end.

For example, to subtract 1.458 from 3.2:
$$\begin{array}{r} 3.2 \\ 1.458 \\ 3.200 \\ -\ 1.458 \\ \hline 1.742 \end{array}$$

Multiply two decimal numbers as if they were large integers, again arranging them vertically and adding trailing zeroes for the number with less decimal places. After all numbers have been multiplied and added together, apply the decimal point to this result. This can be determined by counting the number of decimal places in each factor and adding them together. This will be the number of decimal places in the product, applied by counting places moving right to left.

Division of two decimal numbers is performed like long division on integers, with adjustments for the decimals. If the divisor is a decimal number, move the decimal to the right until no decimal places remain. Next, move the decimal place for the dividend the same number of places (adding zeroes if necessary, to the end of the number.) Then complete the long division.

Finally, the questions in this section will cover rounding numbers to a given decimal place (e.g. to the nearest whole number, or to the nearest hundredth.) Decimals can be rounded by locating the decimal place to round to, and assessing the number to the right of that digit. If the number is below 5, the decimal will be rounded down. For example, rounding 2.54 to the tenths place yields 2.5 (the 4 rounds down to 0.) If the number is at or above 5, the decimal will be rounded up. For example, rounding 2.938 to the nearest hundredth yields 2.94 (the 3 rounds up to 4 because of the 8.)

COMPUTATION WITH DECIMAL NUMBERS QUESTIONS

1. $8.31 + 6.7 + 1.889 =$

    a. 15.899

    b. 16.89

    c. 16.899

    d. 17.89

2. $12.94 \times 5.8 =$

    a. 64.952

    b. 75.052

    c. 649.52

    d. 750.52

3. Round 94.542 to the nearest tenth.

    a. 94.5

    b. 94.55

    c. 94.6

    d. 95

4. $(45.7 - 58.2) \times 0 \times (4.69 \div 1.34) =$

    a. −68

    b. −55.5

    c. 0

    d. 68

5. $14.32 - 12.915 =$

    a. 1.405

    b. 1.414

    c. 2.17

    d. 2.405

Problems Involving Percents

This section covers problems involving percents. A "percent" is some number out of 100. For example, 85% (read "eighty-five percent") means 85 out of 100, which is equivalent to the fraction $\frac{85}{100}$. Percents can be expressed as any positive number, including decimals, fractions, and values larger than 100. The five numbers shown below are all examples of percents:

$$1{,}589\% \qquad \frac{3}{5}\% \qquad \frac{97}{100}\% \qquad 0.8\% \qquad 519.2301\%$$

To answer the questions in this section correctly, students must understand what "percent" means, how to identify a percent, and also how to convert percents to fractions or decimal numbers.

A percent can be converted to a fraction by placing the number over 100 as shown above. While the result is a fraction that is equal to the original percent, it may not be expressed in lowest terms. Put it in lowest terms by dividing the numerator and denominator by their greatest common factor (GCF.)

For example, you can use this process to write 85% as a fraction in lowest terms:

$$85\% = \frac{85}{100}$$
$$= \frac{17}{20}$$

The reverse process can be used to convert a fraction to a percent. If the denominator is 100, convert it to a percent by removing the denominator and adding a percent sign (%) to the numerator. If the denominator is not 100, convert the fraction first to a decimal by dividing the numerator by the denominator. The decimal can be converted to a percent by multiplying it by 100, or equivalently, moving the decimal point two places to the right and then adding a percent sign (%.)

A percent can be converted to a decimal by dividing the percent value by 100 and removing the percent sign (%), or equivalently, move the decimal two places to the left. For example, the percent 52.48% and the decimal 0.5248 are equal.

This section also contains problems that require calculation of value given a percent.

For example, calculate 40% of 62. The word "of" means multiplication, so to find 40% of 62, write it as a multiplication problem:
$$40\% \times 62$$
Then calculate the product by converting 40% to either a fraction or decimal and multiplying the two numbers together:
$$40\% \times 62 = 0.4 \times 62$$
$$= 24.8$$
Thus, 40% of 62 is 24.8.

This section also contains problems that require calculation of a percentage from a given value, such as "What percent of 40 is 35?" or equivalently, "35 is what percent of 40?" The easiest way to solve problems like this is to think of a percent as a part divided by the whole (i.e. $\frac{\text{part}}{\text{whole}}$). The

20

example above states that 35 is some percent of 40, or "35 parts out of 40." Therefore, in terms of the fraction $\frac{\text{part}}{\text{whole}}$, the part is 35 and the whole is 40. Plug these values into this fraction, divide, and then convert the decimal to a percentage as shown below:

$$\frac{\text{part}}{\text{whole}} = \frac{35}{40}$$

$$= 0.875$$

$$= 87.5\%$$

PROBLEMS INVOLVING PERCENTS QUESTIONS

1. **What is 56% of 25?**
   a. 10
   b. 11
   c. 12
   d. 14

2. **Write 45% as a fraction in lowest terms.**
   a. $\frac{2}{5}$
   b. $\frac{9}{20}$
   c. $\frac{4}{5}$
   d. $\frac{20}{9}$

3. **What percent of 56 is 42?**
   a. 60%
   b. 72.5%
   c. 75%
   d. 85%

4. **A school has 48 boys and 72 girls. What percent of the students are boys?**
   a. 30%
   b. 35%
   c. 40%
   d. 45%

5. **What is $\frac{1}{2}$% of 40?**
   a. 0.2
   b. 2
   c. 8
   d. 20

Estimation, Ordering, Number Sense

This section covers how to correctly estimate numbers, put numbers in order from least to greatest, and use mathematical intuition to quickly and accurately solve problems. When solving problems using arithmetic, it is good idea to have a ballpark estimate of the answer. That way, if an answer is much larger or smaller than the estimate, a re-check of the work can be done to see if there was a mistake.

Estimation means approximating the result of a mathematical operation. Because it involves an approximation, estimation is a lot like rounding but extends this idea to include mathematical operations like addition, multiplication, exponents, and square roots, rather than just single numbers. In general, estimating mathematical expressions saves time. Although an estimated answer will not be exact, it can be found much more quickly than an exact answer.

To estimate the sum or difference of two numbers, first round the numbers to a reasonable place (the larger the rounding place, the less accurate the result.) All numbers should be rounded to the same decimal place even if it seems inappropriate for some of them. Next, add or subtract the result.

> For example, to add 578,239 and 89,198, round them to the nearest hundred thousand and then add the result.
> $$578{,}239 + 89{,}198 \approx 600{,}000 + 100{,}000$$
> $$\approx 700{,}000$$

To estimate the product or quotient of two numbers, round each number to their first significant decimal place. In other words, round each number to the first decimal place that is not a zero. Then multiply or divide the rounded numbers.

> For example:
> $$5093 \times 73 \approx 5000 \times 70$$
> $$\approx 350{,}000$$

This process exploits the fact that multiplying and dividing by powers of 10 is relatively easy in the decimal system. For instance, to multiply two very large numbers with lots of trailing zeroes (trailing zeroes are zeroes at the end of a number), multiply the parts that aren't zeroes and then add in all the trailing zeroes at the end.

Estimating the square root of a number is done by finding its nearest perfect square. A perfect square is a positive integer that can be written as the square of another number. For instance, 16 and 100 are both perfect squares since $4^2 = 16$ and $10^2 = 100$. The square root of a perfect square is always a whole number. To estimate the square root of a number, round the original number to its nearest perfect square and then take the square root of that value.

Questions in this section will also require that lists of different types of numbers be placed in order from least to greatest. First, convert all the numbers to the same format (fractions, decimals, percents with the same denominator, etc.) if this not already the case. Next, arrange the numbers in order. If they are all decimals, compare the digits in like decimal place starting with leftmost place and working toward the right. Note that negative numbers are smaller than positive numbers and if the absolute value of a negative number is greater than the absolute value of another negative

22

number, then the first one is smaller than the second. For example, −56 is smaller than −12 because 56 > 12 and 56 is further away on the number line from zero.

Number sense is the phrase used for a person's intuition for numbers and magnitudes. It involves a wide range of concepts, including estimation, rounding, ordering, comparison, and measurement. Consequently, there is no one set of instructions that can be used for all questions involving number sense.

ESTIMATION, ORDERING, NUMBER SENSE QUESTIONS

1. **Estimate the square root of 82.**
   a. 7
   b. 8
   c. 9
   d. 10

2. **Estimate $80,389 \times 597.39$.**
   a. 400,000
   b. 4,800,000
   c. 40,000,000
   d. 48,000,000

3. **Order 1.71, $\frac{8}{5}$, −2, and 1.685 from least to greatest.**
   a. $-2, \frac{8}{5}, 1.685, 1.71$
   b. $-2, 1.685, \frac{8}{5}, 1.71$
   c. $1.685, \frac{8}{5}, 1.71, -2$
   d. $\frac{8}{5}, 1.685, 1.71, -2$

4. **Which of the following is closest to the sum of $\frac{47}{45}$ and $\frac{20}{21}$?**
   a. $\frac{436}{315}$
   b. 1.53
   c. 2
   d. 4

5. **Which of the following is the greatest?**
   a. 24.1% of 120
   b. 34.2% of 99
   c. 49.4% of 72
   d. 51.1% of 90

Word Problems and Applications

This section covers the usage of arithmetic skills to solve word problems. To be successful in this section, you must be able to correctly interpret information given to you in words and apply the various skills of arithmetic, including performing calculations with integers, fractions, percents and decimal numbers, estimating the result of a calculation, and using number sense.

Word problems ask questions about real-life situations. The first step in solving a word problem is to interpret the information given in the problem and formulate a plan to answer the question. This will almost certainly involve performing at least one calculation using numbers in the text, and possibly multiple calculations will be needed to solve the problem.

It is a good idea to carefully reread the problem at the end to make sure the expression created to solve the word problem is accurate and complete.

WORD PROBLEMS AND APPLICATIONS QUESTIONS

1. A school has 300 students, and three-fifths of the students are girls. How many girls attend the school?

   a. 140 girls
   b. 150 girls
   c. 180 girls
   d. 200 girls

2. Jerry goes to the grocery store and pays $2.55 for milk, $3.79 for oranges, and $3.09 for eggs. If he gives the cashier a $20 bill, what will his change be?

   a. $10.57
   b. $10.72
   c. $11.27
   d. $11.62

3. Nancy pays 5% sales tax on a car that costs $25,000. What is the cost of the car including sales tax?

   a. $26,250
   b. $26,800
   c. $27,200
   d. $28,000

4. A school has 270 boys and 450 girls. What percentage of the student body are boys?

   a. 25%
   b. 37.5%
   c. 42.5%
   d. 60%

5. A company sold 810,602 computers last year for $895 each. How much was the total revenue for the computers, approximately?

   a. $56 million
   b. $72 million
   c. $560 million
   d. $720 million

24

Elementary Algebra

Real Numbers

This section measures your ability to correctly identify and manipulate real numbers. Any number that can be represented by a decimal number (including those with an infinite number of digits after the decimal point) is a real number. Visually, you can think of the real numbers as those numbers that can be represented by a point on a number line extending infinitely in both directions from zero.

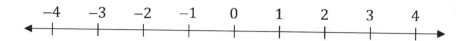

Numbers that are not real are known as imaginary numbers. These numbers are rarely used in everyday math. They are typically found in higher level scientific applications, such as quantum mechanics. Imaginary numbers are real numbers multiplied by the imaginary unit, represented with the symbol i, such as $5i$, and are not covered in this workbook.

The set of real numbers is divided into two groups, rational numbers and irrational numbers. A rational numbers is a number that can be written as a fraction. Here, the word *rational* comes from the fact that the number can be written as the *ratio* of two integers. Included in this set are integers, fractions, and mixed numbers. In addition, two types of decimal numbers are also rational: those that terminate, and those that repeat. Terminating decimals are rational decimal numbers that eventually terminate or end, and repeating decimals are rational decimal numbers that repeat indefinitely. The five numbers below are all examples of rational numbers because they can all be written as fractions:

$$\frac{100}{3} \qquad -5 \qquad 11\frac{4}{9} \qquad 43.913 \qquad -0.9155155155\ldots$$

Irrational numbers, on the other hand, are real numbers that cannot be written as a fraction. Some examples of irrational numbers are square root radicals (which are discussed below) and often-used constants like π (the Greek letter "pi") and e. In fact, any non-terminating, non-repeating decimal is an irrational number.

This section includes problems that involve addition, subtraction, multiplication, and division of real numbers. As a result, students must be comfortable performing these four operations using the correct order of operations. Students should already be familiar with calculations involving fractions and decimal numbers from arithmetic, but they may be less familiar with calculations involving square root radicals.

A square root radical is a number such as $\sqrt{5}$, in other words, one that contains the radical sign ($\sqrt{}$). The number under the radical sign is called the radicand of the number. Additionally, some square root radicals have a coefficient, which is a number before the radical sign that is multiplied by the radical. For example, in $4\sqrt{7}$, 4 is a coefficient of the radical. If a coefficient is not shown on a radical, the coefficient is assumed to be 1 since one times any number is the number itself.

Square root radicals can be added or subtracted through a process called combining "like" radicals. Like radicals are radicals with the same radicand, for example, $2\sqrt{3}$ and $\sqrt{3}$. To combine like radicals, add or subtract their coefficients and keep the radicand the same:

$$2\sqrt{3} + \sqrt{3} = 2\sqrt{3} + 1\sqrt{3}$$
$$= 3\sqrt{3}$$

On the other hand, square root radicals can be multiplied or divided, even if they are not like radicals. Multiply or divide the coefficients (if there are any) and then do the same for the radicands:

$$3\sqrt{5} \times 2\sqrt{11} = 6\sqrt{55}$$

In this example, the result cannot be simplified. But, in some cases, the product or quotient of two radicals may be simplified further.

To simplify a square root radical, check to see if the radicand is a perfect square. A perfect square is a positive integer that is the square of an integer, so numbers like 16 and 100 are perfect squares because $4^2 = 16$ and $10^2 = 100$. If the radicand of a square root radical is a perfect square, simplify by taking its square root.

If the radicand is not a perfect square, rewrite the radicand as the product of two numbers, the greatest perfect square factor (if one exists) and another factor.

For instance, simplify $\sqrt{45}$ by factoring 9, a perfect square factor, and 5:
$$\sqrt{45} = \sqrt{9 \times 5}$$
Next separate the result into two radicals using these factors:
$$\sqrt{9 \times 5} = \sqrt{9} \times \sqrt{5}$$
Finally, take the square root of the first factor. The result will be a square root radical with a coefficient.
$$\sqrt{9} \times \sqrt{5} = 3\sqrt{5}$$

REAL NUMBERS QUESTIONS

1. Which of the following numbers is an irrational number?

    a. -5

    b. $-\frac{11}{8}$

    c. $0.\overline{33}$

    d. π

2. $\left(\frac{2}{3} - \frac{1}{4}\right) \div \frac{1}{4} =$

    a. $\frac{5}{48}$

    b. $\frac{1}{3}$

    c. $\frac{5}{3}$

    d. 48

3. $\dfrac{4.8 - 12.3}{-1 - 4} =$

    a. −2.5

    b. −1.5

    c. 1.5

    d. 2.5

4. $\sqrt{63} =$

    a. $3\sqrt{7}$

    b. $7\sqrt{3}$

    c. $7\sqrt{9}$

    d. $9\sqrt{7}$

5. $\sqrt{3} \times \sqrt{7} =$

    a. 3

    b. $\sqrt{21}$

    c. 10

    d. 21

Linear Equations, Inequalities and Systems

This section measures the ability to correctly solve linear equations, linear inequalities, and systems of linear equations. Here, the word *linear* refers to the fact that the equations can be graphically represented with a line. Symbolically, a linear equation is an equation of degree 1, and thus an equation whose highest degree is 1. The degree of a monomial is defined as the sum of the exponents of each of its variables. For example, the degree of $4a^3b^6$ is 9 because $3 + 6 = 9$. Therefore, a linear equation is an equation in which every monomial either has degree 0 (i.e. a constant) or degree 1 (i.e. a term with one variable whose exponent is 1.)

The solution to a linear equation is the number that satisfies the equation. In other words, if you substitute the solution for all occurrences of the variable in the equation, the result will be a true equality. For instance, $x = 5$ is the solution to the equation $x + 2 = 7$ because substitution of 5 for x results in a true equality, $5 + 2 = 7$. Generally speaking, a linear equation with one variable will have one and only one solution.

Two equations are considered equivalent if they have the same solution. For example, the equations, $4x = 12$ and $x - 1 = 2$, are equivalent because they both have the solution $x = 3$. Writing a series of equivalent equations can produce a solution for any linear equation. Start with a given equation, then using the basic rules of algebra, transform it through a series of equivalent equation until you finally reach an equation of the form *variable = number* (or vice versa). This number is the solution to the original equation.

Equations can be transformed using any of the rules for manipulating expressions, including distributing over parentheses; performing calculations with integers, fractions, decimals, and radicals; combining like terms; simplifying exponents; and so on. Notice that these rules only apply to expressions and thus can only be used to affect terms on one side of the equals sign. Consequently, they are of no use if you want to make changes to both sides of the equation.

However, any operation can be applied to one side of the equation as long as the same operation is applied to the other side as well.

For example, to solve the equation $3c = 6$, both sides can be divided by 3 and then simplified:

$$3c = 6$$
$$\frac{3c}{3} = \frac{6}{3}$$
$$c = 2$$

Some operations do not follow this rule (e.g. squaring both sides of an equation), but do not apply when solving linear equations.

To solve a linear equation with one variable, first simplify both sides of the equation.

For example, to solve the equation $3(x + 2) = 0$, first distribute the 3 on the left side:

$$3(x + 2) = 0$$
$$3x + 6 = 0$$

After both sides are simplified, isolate the variable on one side of the equation. A variable is said to be isolated if it appears alone (save for a coefficient) on one side of the equation and does not

28

appear at all on the other side. Any term can be "moved" from one side of the equation to the other by subtracting it from both sides, or equivalently, by adding its opposite. In the example above, the term $3x$ is isolated by subtracting 6 from both sides:

$$3x + 6 = 0$$
$$(3x + 6) - 6 = 0 - 6$$
$$3x = -6$$

The resulting equation can be solved for x by dividing both sides by the coefficient of the variable term, which is 3:

$$3x = -6$$
$$\frac{3x}{3} = \frac{-6}{3}$$
$$x = -2$$

Always validate a solution by substituting the value back into the original equation and confirming that it satisfies the equation. For the example above, substitute -2 for x into the original equation:

$$3(x + 2) = 0$$
$$3[(-2) + 2] = 0$$
$$3(0) = 0$$

Since the result is a true equality, the solution $x = -2$ is correct.

Inequalities are similar to equations, but instead of an equals sign, they have an inequality sign (either $>, <, \geq, \leq,$ or $\neq$.) Linear inequalities are solved in the same way as linear equations. The only difference is that when multiplying or dividing by a negative number, the inequality sign must be flipped (i.e. $>$ becomes $<$, $\geq$ becomes $\leq$.)

For example, the inequality $-3t < 6$ can be solved by dividing both sides by -3, then flipping the inequality sign:

$$-3t < 6$$
$$\frac{-3t}{-3} > \frac{6}{-3}$$
$$t > -2$$

Recall that a linear equation is an equation in which none of the variables have exponents greater than 1. However, a linear equation can have multiple variables. If it does, the equation may not necessarily have one numerical solution. In fact, to solve an equation with more than one variable requires more than one equation. Specifically, if given two variables, there must be two equations to solve; if three variables, then three equations are needed, etc.

A set of multiple linear equations with multiple variables is called a system of linear equations. Because a system of linear equations has multiple variables, its solution will be a list of values for each variable in the system. For instance, the solution to the system of equations shown below is $a = 1$ and $b = 3$; substituting both values into the equations below will result in two true equalities:

$$a + b = 4$$

$$a - b = -2$$

There are two methods for solving a system of linear equations: substitution and elimination. The substitution method is convenient to use when one of the equations is in the form *variable = expression* (or vice versa), and the isolated variable does not appear anywhere on the other side. For instance, in the linear system below, the first equation is in this form, so the substitution method can be used to solve it:

$$x = 4y - 1$$

$$2x - 3 = 3y$$

Solve this system by substituting $4y - 1$ for x into the second equation:

$$2(4y - 1) - 3 = 3y$$

Since the result is a linear equation with one variable, it can be solved for y using the process for solving a single variable linear equation. Once the value of y is found, substitute that value in either original equation and solve for the other variable, *x*.

Unfortunately, substitution is convenient for only a relatively limited number of situations. In many cases, a method called elimination (or combining equations) will be faster. To use the elimination method, add or subtract two equations in order to eliminate a variable. Linear systems like the example below are ideal candidates for the elimination method because the term $3n$ appears in the first equation and its opposite, $-3n$, is in the second equation:

$$4m + 3n = 5$$

$$m - 3n = 5$$

Adding the two equations together will cause the *n*-terms to cancel out:

$$4m + 3n = 5$$
$$\underline{m - 3n = 5}$$
$$5m + 0 = 10$$

As with the substitution method, the result is a linear equation with one variable, so it can be solved for *m* using the process discussed above. Substitute the value for *m* in either original equation and solve the result for *n*.

For a system of equations in which the coefficients of the variables are not opposites, the elimination method can still be used by multiplying one or more of the equations by a constant to get the coefficients into this form. In the example below, multiplying the first equation by 2 and the second equation by 3, will yield coefficients of the *x*-terms that will be opposites which can be added and cancelled:

$$3x + 5y = -1 \qquad 2(3x + 5y = -1) \qquad 6x + 10y = -2$$
$$-2x + 6y = 10 \qquad 3(-2 + 6y = 10) \qquad -6x + 18y = 30$$

LINEAR EQUATIONS, INEQUALITIES AND SYSTEMS QUESTIONS

1. If $2 - 4(x + 3) = 6$, then $x = ?$

    a. -4
    b. -1
    c. 1
    d. 4

2. If $3a = 2a + a + 4a - 4$, then $a = ?$

    a. 0
    b. 1
    c. $\frac{5}{2}$
    d. 3

3. Which of the following expressions is equivalent to $4 - \frac{1}{3}y > 5$?

    a. $y < -27$
    b. $y < -3$
    c. $y > -3$
    d. $y > 27$

4. If $x + 3y = 3$ and $-x + y = 5$, then $x = ?$

    a. -3
    b. -2
    c. 2
    d. 3

5. If $x = 2y - 3$ and $2x + \frac{1}{2}y = 3$, then $y = ?$

    a. $-\frac{2}{3}$
    b. 1
    c. 2
    d. $\frac{18}{7}$

Quadratic Expressions and Equations

This section measures the ability to correctly manipulate quadratic expressions and solve quadratic equations. Quadratic expressions are special types of expressions built out of monomials and polynomials.

A monomial is a single number, a variable, or the product of one or more numbers and variables with positive integer exponents. For example, the terms $\sqrt{3}$ and $\frac{4}{7}ab^5$ are both monomials, whereas the terms $\frac{4}{x^2}$ and $t^{\frac{3}{2}}$ are not since $\frac{4}{x^2}$ contains division by a variable, and $t^{\frac{3}{2}}$ has a non-integer exponent.

A series of multiple monomials separated by addition and subtraction signs form a type of expression called a polynomial. The expressions shown below are both examples of polynomials because all of their terms are valid monomials:

$$\frac{2}{3}xy^5z - \pi x^2 + 4 \qquad 2a^4 + 0.05a^3 - a^2 - 12.1a + 3$$

If a polynomial contains two monomials, it is called a binomial. If a polynomial contains three monomials, it is called a trinomial.

This section focused on how to manipulate quadratic expressions and equations. A quadratic expression is a polynomial of degree 2. In other words, it is a polynomial whose highest degree is 2. The degree of a monomial is defined as the sum of all the exponents on its variables. For example, the degree of $5xy^4z^2$ is 7 because $1 + 4 + 2 = 7$. Therefore, a quadratic expression is an expression in which every monomial either has degree 0, 1, or 2. Furthermore, a quadratic equation is an equation constructed only of quadratic expressions.

Any of the four main operations (addition, subtraction, multiplication, and division) can be performed on two or more polynomials. Two polynomials can be added or subtracted by setting up the operation vertically, aligning like terms, and then adding or subtracting like terms.

To multiply a constant by a polynomial, use the distributive property. Although the distributive property is usually given in the form $a(b + c) = ab + ac$, it can be extended to include polynomials with many monomials. For example, to distribute the expression $3(2a^3 + a^2 - 7)$, multiply the 3 by the coefficient of each term inside the parentheses and then simplify the result:

$$3(2a^3 + a^2 - 7) = (3 \cdot 2a^3) + (3 \cdot a^2) + [3 \cdot (-7)]$$

$$= 6a^3 + 3a^2 - 21$$

To multiply two binomials together, use the "FOIL" method. FOIL is an acronym that stands for "First, Outer, Inner, Last." This specifies the four products that must be calculated in order to complete the multiplication. First multiply the first terms of the binomial, then multiply the outer terms of the binomials, then multiply the inner terms of the binomials, and finally multiply the last terms of the binomials. Rules for multiplying terms with positive and/or negative signs must be carefully observed.

For instance, to multiply $(2x - 3)(x + 6)$, calculate the four FOIL products as follows:

The product of the First terms of $(\mathbf{2x} - 3)(\mathbf{x} + 6)$ is $2x \cdot x = 2x^2$.

The product of the Outer terms of $(\mathbf{2x} - 3)(x + \mathbf{6})$ is $2x \cdot 6 = 12x$.

The product of the Inner terms of $(2x - \mathbf{3})(\mathbf{x} + 6)$ is $(-3) \cdot x = -3x$.

The product of the Last terms of $(2x - \mathbf{3})(x + \mathbf{6})$ is $(-3) \cdot 6 = -18$.

Next, add the four products together and simplify the result by combining like terms:

$$(2x - 3)(x + 6) = 2x^2 + 12x - 3x - 18$$
$$= 2x^2 + 9x - 18$$

The opposite of multiplying polynomials is a process called factoring. In this section, some problems will require factoring a trinomial into a product of two binomials. Based on the example above, the factorization of $2x^2 + 9x - 18$ is the product $(2x - 3)(x + 6)$.

When factoring a polynomial, start by determining if the coefficients of the terms have a common factor. If so, find their greatest common factor (GCF) and factor it out. For example, the coefficients of the trinomial in the example below are 4, 16, and −84, which have a GCF of 4. Factor the 4 out by dividing the coefficient of each term by 4 (without changing the variables), and leaving the resulting values in parentheses:

$$4x^2 + 16x - 84 = 4(x^2 + 4x - 21)$$

Notice that the expression in parentheses is a trinomial in the form $ax^2 + bx + c$ with $a = 1$. Trinomials in this form are sometimes able to be factored. If a factorization does exist, it will be the product of two binomials in the form $(x + a)(x + b)$. To find the values of a and b, find two numbers whose sum is the coefficient of the x-term and whose product is the constant, c. In the example above, the coefficient of the x-term is 4 and the constant is −21. Therefore, a and b should be −3 and 7. Substitute these values into the format $(x + a)(x + b)$ to obtain the factorization of the trinomial. This factorization replaces the value in parentheses as shown:

$$4(x^2 + 4x - 21) = 4(x - 3)(x + 7)$$

Trinomials in the form $ax^2 + bx + c$ can sometimes be factored even if a > 1. In this case the factorization will be the product of two binomials in the form $(ax + b)(cx + d)$. The values of a, b, c, and d can be found using trial-and-error. For a and c, consider all integer combinations whose product is the coefficient of the x^2-term. Similarly, for b and d, consider all integer combinations whose product is the constant, c. For instance, to factor the trinomial $9x^2 + 6x - 8$, the following combinations may be tried:

$$(3x + 8)(3x - 1) = 9x^2 + 21x - 8$$

$$(9x + 4)(x - 2) = 9x^2 - 14x - 8$$

Unfortunately, neither combination is correct since neither gives $6x$ as the middle term of the trinomial. Continuing with possible combinations will yield the following correct factorization of the trinomial:

$$9x^2 + 6x - 8 = (3x + 4)(3x - 2)$$

In addition, you can also factor binomials if they are the difference of two squares. A binomial is said to be the difference of two squares if it is in the form $a^2 - b^2$. For instance, $4c^2 - 81$ is the difference of two squares because the first term, $4c^2$, is the square of $2c$ and the second term, 81, is the square of 9. Factor binomials in this form using the rule $a^2 - b^2 = (a - b)(a + b)$:

$$4c^2 - 81 = (2c - 9)(2c + 9)$$

Lastly, this section will include questions that involve solving quadratic equations. Most of the time, quadratic equations will have two possible solutions. To solve a quadratic equation, move all the terms to one side and simplify the result. The result will be an equation in the form *quadratic expression = 0*. Next factor the expression on the left side using one of the methods described above.

Once the expression is factored, solve it by using the zero-product rule. The zero-product rule states that if the product of two expressions is zero, then one of the expressions must be zero. In other words, once the equation is factored, set each factor equal to zero and solve the resulting equation.

For example, to solve the equation $4c^2 - 81 = 0$, factor the quadratic expression on the left side, then set each factor equal to zero and solve those equations.

$$4c^2 - 81 = 0$$
$$(2c - 9)(2c + 9) = 0$$
$$2c - 9 = 0$$
$$c = \frac{9}{2}$$
$$\text{or}$$
$$2c + 9 = 0$$
$$c = -\frac{9}{2}$$

Therefore, the possible solutions to the equation are $c = -\frac{9}{2}$ and $c = \frac{9}{2}$. Each solution must be verified by plugging the value into the original equation. In this case, both are valid solutions.

QUADRATIC EXPRESSIONS AND EQUATIONS QUESTIONS

1. $\left(y^2 + 9y - 2\right) + \left(4y^2 - y - 5\right) =$
    a. $5y^2 + 8y - 7$
    b. $5y^2 + 8y + 10$
    c. $5y^2 + 10y - 7$
    d. $5y^2 + 10y + 10$

2. $(x + 3)(x - 1) =$

    a. $x^2 - 3$
    b. $x^2 + 2$
    c. $x^2 - 3x + 2$
    d. $x^2 + 2x - 3$

3. $2c^2 - 32 =$

    a. $(c - 16)^2$
    b. $2(c + 4)^2$
    c. $(c - 16)(c + 16)$
    d. $2(c - 4)(c + 4)$

4. If $x^2 + 5x = 6$, then $x = ?$

    a. -6 or -1
    b. -6 or 1
    c. -1 or 6
    d. 1 or 6

5. If $2n^2 + 9n + 4 = 0$, then $n = ?$

    a. -4 or -2
    b. -4 or $-\frac{1}{2}$
    c. -2 or $-\frac{1}{4}$
    d. $-\frac{1}{4}$ or $-\frac{1}{2}$

Algebraic Expressions and Equations

This section measures the ability to correctly manipulate algebraic expressions and equations using the rules of algebra. A significant part of this requires an understanding of the basic concepts of algebra and its terminology. One of the most fundamental concepts in algebra is the concept of a variable.

A variable is a symbol that represents an unknown quantity. Variables are typically represented by English letters such as a, b, c, x, and y. In some contexts, Greek letters like α and θ are used. Conversely, a constant is a specific number or value such as 4.5, $-\frac{97}{203}$, or $2\sqrt{3}$. Some often-used numbers (e.g. π and e) are represented by letters even though they are constants, not variables.

The combination of variables and constants connected by one or more arithmetic operations form something called an algebraic expression. Expressions can appear in a wide variety of forms as the five examples below demonstrate:

$$5x \qquad 9a + \frac{7}{2}b - 4 \qquad 63.2m^4n \div \pi \qquad \frac{5}{z^{1/2}} \qquad 9\sqrt{t} - u$$

Expressions can be divided into smaller subunits called terms. For instance, the expression $9a + \frac{7}{2}b - 4$ is made up of three terms, $9a$, $\frac{7}{2}b$, and 4 that are separated by addition or subtraction signs. The number at the beginning of a term with a variable is called its coefficient. The coefficient of $9a$ is 9, and the coefficient of $\frac{7}{2}b$ is the fraction $\frac{7}{2}$. When the coefficient is not shown, it is equal to 1 since one times any number is the number itself.

An expression does not contain an equal sign (=) or an inequality sign ($>$, $<$, $\geq$, $\leq$, or $\neq$.) These signs indicate an equation or an inequality, not an expression; equations and inequalities can be solved for an unknown value whereas expressions alone cannot. An equation (or inequality) is really a pair of expressions separated by an equal sign (or inequality sign.) Each expression on either side of the equal sign can be referenced as the left side or the right side of the equation.

The questions in this section involve algebraic expressions that contain one or more variables. In addition to the rules of arithmetic for performing calculations with numbers, this section requires manipulation of variables, terms, expressions, and equations. In particular, this section will test ability to evaluate algebraic expressions and determine whether a solution satisfies an equation.

An algebraic expression can be evaluated if numerical values are provided for each of its variables. To evaluate an expression, substitute the corresponding value for each occurrence of the variable and then calculate the result.

For instance, if $x = 3$ and $y = 5$, then the expression $\frac{2x^2y}{8-2x}$ can be evaluated as follows:

$$\frac{2x^2y}{8-2x} = \frac{2(3)^2(5)}{8-2(3)}$$
$$= \frac{2 \cdot 9 \cdot 5}{8 - 6}$$
$$= \frac{90}{2}$$
$$= 45$$

Along the same lines, a solution is said to satisfy an equation if evaluating the equation for that value results in a true equality. For example, the solution $a = 1$ satisfies the equation $2a = 2$ because when 1 is substituted for a in the equation, the result is $2 \cdot 1 = 2$, which is true.

In addition, this section will also test application of the four main operations (addition, subtraction, multiplication, division, and exponentiation) on algebraic terms.

Algebraic terms can only be added or subtracted if they are *like terms*. *Like terms* are terms that contain the same variables with the same exponents on the variables. The coefficients of the terms may differ, however. For instance, x^6y and $0.2yx^6$ are like terms because they both contain the variables x^6 and y. Like terms can be combined by adding or subtracting their coefficients and keeping the variables and exponents the same:

$$x^6y - 0.2yx^6 = 1x^6y - 0.2x^6y$$

$$= 0.8x^6y$$

On the other hand, any two terms can be multiplied or divided, even if they are not like terms. To do this, multiply corresponding parts of the terms (i.e. the coefficients and like variables) separately as in $2a \cdot 3ab = (2 \cdot 3)(a \cdot a)b = 6a^2b$. Even a constant and a term with a variable can be multiplied or divided (since constants are terms, too) by multiplying or dividing the constant by the coefficient of the term. After multiplication or division of terms, use one or more of the exponent rules to simplify the result.

An exponent (also called a power) is an operation that represents a constant or variable multiplied by itself some number of times (the value of the exponent.) For instance, 2^5 (read "two to the fifth power") means you multiply 2 by itself five times. In this example, 2 is referred to as the base of exponent, and 5 is the exponent itself. Similarly, a^6 means you multiply a by itself six times. By default, any variable without an exponent, has a power of 1 which means the value is just the variable itself.

Exponents can be applied to entire terms or expressions, not just single variables. In these situations, the exponent is distributed to each constant or variable within the expression (inside the parentheses.)

In the example below, this means that multiplying $6mn^2$ by itself four times is the same thing as distributing the exponent 4 among the three parts of the expression in parentheses, 6, m, and n^2:

$$(6mn^2)^4 = (6mn^2)(6mn^2)(6mn^2)(6mn^2)$$
$$= (6 \cdot 6 \cdot 6 \cdot 6)(m \cdot m \cdot m \cdot m)(n^2 \cdot n^2 \cdot n^2 \cdot n^2)$$
$$= 6^4 \cdot m^4 \cdot (n^2)^4$$

In addition to this, there are three main exponent rules that you should know for this section that will help you simplify expressions containing an exponent. First, to multiply exponential expressions with the same base, keep the base the same and add the exponents. For instance, since t^4 and t^2 have the same base, you can multiply them by adding their exponents:

$$t^4 \cdot t^2 = t^{4+2}$$

$$= t^6$$

Similarly, to divide exponential expressions with the same base, do the same thing, except subtract the exponents instead of adding them. Thus, to divide y^8 by y^3, subtract 3 from 8 and use the result as the new exponent of y:

$$y^8 \div y^3 = y^{8-3}$$
$$= y^5$$

Third, to raise an exponential expression to a power, multiply the two exponents together. For example, to raise a^3 to the fifth power, multiply 3 by 5:

$$(a^3)^5 = a^{3 \cdot 5}$$
$$= a^{15}$$

Finally, there is one more rule of algebra required to complete the problems in this section. To multiply a term by an expression that contains more than one term, distribute the first term over every term in the expression. In other words, multiply the first term by each term in the expression and then simplify the result. For instance, to simplify $-4a(5x - 2)$, distribute the $-4a$ by multiplying it by each term in parentheses (i.e. $5x$ and -2):

$$-4a(5x - 2) = (-4a \cdot 5x) + [-4a \cdot (-2)]$$
$$= -20ax + 8a$$

When distributing, it is crucial to keep track of the positive and negative signs of every term. Students often make the mistake of distributing the example above by either losing the negative sign on $-4a$ when multiplying it by -2 or losing the negative sign on -2:

$$-4a(5x - 2) \neq (-4a \cdot 5x) + [4a \cdot (-2)]$$
$$-4a(5x - 2) \neq (-4a \cdot 5x) + (-4a \cdot 2)$$

Either mistake will give the result $-20ax - 8a$, which is incorrect.

ALGEBRAIC EXPRESSIONS AND EQUATIONS QUESTIONS

1. What is the value of $2x^2 + 5x - y^2$ when $x = 3$ and $y = 5$?

    a. -4
    b.   8
    c.   16
    d.   72

2. Which of the following solutions satisfies the equation $5x = 15$?

    a. $x = 2$
    b. $x = 3$
    c. $x = 5$
    d. $x = 10$

3. If $a \neq 0$, then $12a^2b \div 3a = ?$

    a. $4b$

    b. $4ab$

    c. $9b^2$

    d. $9ab$

4. $(4x^5)^2 =$

    a. $4x^{10}$

    b. $4x^{25}$

    c. $8x^{25}$

    d. $16x^{10}$

5. $4x + 3(2y - x) =$

    a. $x + 6y$

    b. $3x + 6y$

    c. $4x + 3y$

    d. $7xy$

Word Problems and Applications

This section measures the ability to correctly use the algebraic skills tested so far in the form of word problems. This requires correctly interpreting information given in sentence format and using the skills tested in the rest of the section, including performing calculations with real numbers, manipulating and evaluating algebraic expressions, and solving linear and quadratic equations.

Word problems ask questions about real-life situations. The first step is to interpret the information given in the problem and formulate a plan to answer the question. In the most straightforward case, this plan may just involve performing a calculation with real numbers. But more likely, a multi-step process must be used, creating variables for an unknown number, setting up an equation containing that variable, solving the equation, and then interpreting the solution in the context of the original word problem. In some instances, a system of multiple equations each having multiple variables may be needed, which can be solved using either the elimination method or the substitution method.

After solving a word problem, it is a good idea to carefully reread the original problem to make sure that the solution took into account all necessary information, and is a valid solution. Be certain to provide the exact information requested in the word problem.

WORD PROBLEMS AND APPLICATIONS QUESTIONS

1. The volume of a rectangular box is found by multiplying its length, width, and height. If the dimensions of a box are $\sqrt{3}$, $2\sqrt{5}$, and 4, what is its volume?

   a. $2\sqrt{60}$
   b. $4\sqrt{15}$
   c. $8\sqrt{15}$
   d. $24\sqrt{5}$

2. A cab ride costs $3.60 for the first half-mile and $0.75 for each additional mile. If d represents the distance travelled in miles, which expression represents the total cost of the cab ride in dollars?

   a. $2.85 + 0.75d$
   b. $2.85 + 0.75(d - 0.5)$
   c. $3.60 + 0.75d$
   d. $3.60 + 0.75(d - 0.5)$

3. Adam has 24 coins worth $3.30. If the coins consist of dimes and quarters, how many dimes does Adam have?

   a. 6 dimes
   b. 10 dimes
   c. 16 dimes
   d. 18 dimes

4. The length of Square A is 3 feet longer than the length of Square B. If the difference between their areas is 75 ft², what is the length of Square B?

   a. 11 feet
   b. 12 feet
   c. 13 feet
   d. 14 feet

5. A metal ball is thrown up in the air from an initial height of 3 feet. Its height above the ground, in feet, t seconds after it is thrown is given by the expression $-16t^2 + 47t + 3$. How long will it take (in seconds) for the ball to hit the ground after it is thrown?

   a. $\frac{1}{16}$ seconds

   b. 1 second

   c. 3 seconds

   d. $4\frac{1}{2}$ seconds

College Level Mathematics

Algebraic Operations

This section measures the ability to simplify the result of various algebraic operations, including multiplication and division of polynomials, factoring, exponents, and radicals. Some of the problems in this section will involve concepts such as rational expressions and fractional exponents. In others, these more familiar concepts will be treated in more complicated ways.

Students should know the procedure for factoring trinomials in the form $ax^2 + bx + c$. Substitution can be used to extend this procedure to allow factoring polynomials such as $x^{10} + 6x^5 + 8$, in other words, polynomials whose degree is greater than 2. To use the substitution method, create a temporary variable (traditionally u, but any letter can be used) and set it equal to the variable in the trinomial to a power that is half of the degree of the trinomial. For example, to factor $x^{10} + 6x^5 + 8$, use $u = x^5$ (since 5 is half of 10) for the temporary variable.

Next, substitute u into the equation where possible. The result will be a trinomial whose only variable is u. It may make the substitution easier if the monomial is rewritten before substituting. For example, if $= x^5$, rewrite each monomial to show the x^5 explicitly and only after that would you substitute in u for x^5:

$$x^{10} + 6x^5 + 8 = (x^5)^2 + 6(x^5) + 8$$

$$= u^2 + 6u + 8$$

After substituting, the result will be a trinomial in the form $au^2 + bu + c$. Therefore, if it is factorable, the factorization will be the product of two binomials in the form $(au + b)(cu + d)$:

$$u^2 + 6u + 8 = (u + 2)(u + 4)$$

While this is a correct factorization of the trinomial, the ultimate factorization should not contain the temporary variable since u was only created to make the factorization easier. Eliminate the temporary variable using reverse of the substitution performed before. In this example, substitute x^5 for every occurrence of u in the factorization:

$$(u + 2)(u + 4) = (x^5 + 2)(x^5 + 4)$$

The result is one factorization of the original trinomial. Although it is not the case in this example, it may be possible to factor the result further, for instance if one of the factors is the difference of two squares.

A rational algebraic expression is the quotient of two polynomials. For instance, the expressions $\frac{5x}{8ax+b}$ and $\frac{x^2+5x+6}{3x+6}$ are both rational expressions. Rational expressions are very similar to fractions, except that they contain variables and exponents instead of just integers. A rational expression can be simplified using a method similar to the one used to simplify fractions. Specifically, a rational expression can be simplified by dividing the numerator and denominator by the same expression.

In this technique, that expression must be a factor of both the numerator and denominator. The first step is to factor the numerator and denominator as much as possible. Next, cancel out any common expressions that appear in both the numerator and denominator by dividing them both by the common expression.

For instance, to simplify the rational expression $\frac{x^2+5x+6}{3x+6}$, factor the numerator and denominator and then cancel out the common factor $(x+2)$:

$$\frac{x^2+5x+6}{3x+6} = \frac{(x+3)(x+2)}{3(x+2)}$$
$$= \frac{x+3}{3}$$

The FOIL method (a technique used to multiply two binomials) can be extended to allow you to expand more complicated expressions, such as $(a^2 - 5a)(3a - 2b + 4)$, which is the product of a binomial and a trinomial. To expand the product of two polynomials with any number of terms, multiply each term in the first polynomial by the second polynomial (in its entirety) as in the example below:

$$(a^2 - 5a)(3a - 2b + 4) = a^2(3a - 2b + 4) - 5a(3a - 2b + 4)$$

Next, distribute each product and combine like terms in the result:

$$a^2(3a - 2b + 4) - 5a(3a - 2b + 4)$$
$$= (3a^3 - 2a^2b + 4a^2) + (-15a^2 + 10ab - 20a)$$
$$= 3a^3 - 11a^2 - 20a + 10ab - 2a^2b$$

As with the FOIL method, it is important to keep track of the positive and negative signs throughout the whole process to arrive at the correct result.

Finally, to complete this section, students must be able to manipulate exponents and radicals with greater complexity than in elementary algebra. In particular, students should know how to work with negative exponents and understand the relationship between exponents and roots.

Recall that the reciprocal of an expression is a fraction with 1 in the numerator and the original expression in the denominator. For instance, the reciprocal of m is $\frac{1}{m}$. In addition to that notation, the reciprocal of any expression can be written using an exponent of -1. As an example, the expression m^{-1} is another way to write the reciprocal of m, so $m^{-1} = \frac{1}{m}$. Raising a number or expression to any negative exponent is the same thing as raising it to a positive exponent and then taking the reciprocal of the result: $a^{-4} = \frac{1}{a^4}$.

The word *root* (as in square root) has the same meaning as the word *radical*. The nth root of a number is the number that must be raised to the nth power to get the original number. For instance, the fifth root of 32, written as $\sqrt[5]{32}$, is equal to 2 because $2^5 = 32$. In this example, the 5 is called the degree of the root and 32 is called the radicand.

Any root can be converted to an expression with a rational exponent (and vice versa) by using the rule $a^{\frac{m}{n}} = \left(\sqrt[n]{a}\right)^m = \sqrt[n]{a^m}$. This rule says that when converting a rational exponent to a root, the degree of the root comes from the denominator of the exponent, and the new exponent comes from the numerator. This rule can be used to calculate the value of complicated expressions involving rational exponents like the example below:

$$4^{\frac{3}{2}} = (\sqrt[2]{4})^3$$
$$= 2^3$$
$$= 8$$

ALGEBRAIC OPERATIONS QUESTIONS

1. $y^4 + 3y^2 - 4 =$
   a. $(y^3 - 4)(y + 1)$
   b. $(y^3 + 1)(y - 4)$
   c. $(y^2 + 1)(y - 2)(y + 2)$
   d. $(y^2 + 4)(y - 1)(y + 1)$

2. If $x \neq 5$, then $\frac{x^2 - 3x - 10}{4x - 20} = ?$
   a. $\frac{x-5}{5}$
   b. $\frac{x-2}{4}$
   c. $\frac{x+2}{4}$
   d. $\frac{x^2 - 3x - 10}{4}$

3. $(2n^2 + 3n + 1)^2 =$
   a. $4n^4 + 6n^2 + 2$
   b. $4n^4 + 9n^2 + 1$
   c. $4n^4 + 6n^3 + 4n^2 + 3n + 1$
   d. $4n^4 + 12n^3 + 13n^2 + 6n + 1$

4. $(4a)^{-2} =$
   a. $\frac{1}{4a^2}$
   b. $\frac{1}{16a^2}$
   c. $2\sqrt{a}$
   d. $16\sqrt{a}$

5. $3^{\frac{5}{2}} - 3^{\frac{3}{2}} =$
   a. $3\sqrt{3}$
   b. $3\sqrt{5}$
   c. $6\sqrt{3}$
   d. $6\sqrt{5}$

Solutions of Equations and Inequalities

This section measures the ability to solve different types of equations and inequalities using algebraic methods. This section builds on techniques already developed in elementary algebra, but will focus on algebraic equations and inequalities that require more complicated methods to solve.

To solve a quadratic equation, first move everything to one side of the equation and then try to factor the result. There are three different methods used to factor a quadratic expression: factoring out a monomial, factoring a trinomial in the form $ax^2 + bx + c$ into the product of two binomials, or factoring the difference of two squares.

However, some quadratic equations cannot be factored with any of these methods. If a quadratic equation in the form $ax^2 + bx + c = 0$ cannot be factored, use the quadratic formula to solve it:

$$x = \frac{-b \pm \sqrt{b^2 - 4ac}}{2a}$$

The variables a, b, and c are the coefficients of the original trinomial.

> For instance, to solve the equation $2x^2 - 2x - 7 = 0$, substitute $a = 2$, $b = -2$, and $c = -7$ into the quadratic formula and then simplify the result:
>
> 11
>
> Therefore, the solutions to the equation are $x = \frac{1}{2} - \frac{\sqrt{15}}{2}$ and $x = \frac{1}{2} + \frac{\sqrt{15}}{2}$.

Next, recall that an inequality is a mathematical statement that contains an inequality sign (either >, <, ≥, ≤, or ≠.) In most cases, the solution to a quadratic inequality will be a solution set defined by an inequality (or set of inequalities), such as $-4 < x < 9$ or $x \leq 1$ or $x \geq 7$. To find the solution set of a quadratic equation, the first step is to change the inequality sign to an equal sign (=) and solve the resulting equation by either factoring or using the quadratic formula.

> For instance, solve the inequality $x^2 + x - 2 \leq 0$ by re-writing the inequality as an equation and solving that for x:
> $$x^2 + x - 2 = 0$$
> $$(x + 2)(x - 1) = 0$$
> $$x + 2 = 0 \quad \text{or} \quad x - 1 = 0$$
> $$x = -2 \qquad \qquad x = 1$$

Most quadratic equations have two solutions. These two solutions divide the number line into three regions. In the example above, the two solutions, $x = -2$ and $x = 1$, divide the number line into the three regions: $x < -2$, $-2 < x < 1$, and $x > 1$. To determine which regions are part of the solution set, pick a test value from each and substitute it in the original inequality. If the result is a true inequality, then the whole region is part of the solution set. Otherwise, the whole region is not part in the solution set. For the example, choose the numbers $x = -3$, $x = 0$, and $x = 2$ as the three test values and then test them:

Region	Test Value	$x^2 + x - 2 \leq 0$	Conclusion
$x < -2$	-3	$(-3)^2 + (-3) - 2 \leq 0$ $9 - 3 - 2 \leq 0$ $4 \leq 0$	Not part of the solution set
$-2 < x < 1$	0	$(0)^2 + (0) - 2 \leq 0$ $-2 \leq 0$	Part of the solution set
$x > 1$	2	$(2)^2 + (2) - 2 \leq 0$ $4 + 2 - 2 \leq 0$ $4 \leq 0$	Not part of the solution set

Based upon these results, only one of the regions, $-2 < x < 1$, is part of the solution set. Furthermore, since the original inequality sign was a less-than-or-equal-to sign (rather than just a less-than sign), the solution set contains the points $x = -2$ and $x = 1$ as well. Therefore, the solution set is $-2 \leq x \leq 1$.

A system of equations is a set of multiple linear equations with multiple variables. This section requires solving systems with more than two equations and more than two variables. To solve systems like this, start by organizing the equations by writing them vertically with corresponding variables lined up. Next, label the equations with numbers for reference (e.g. Label the first equation as "equation (1)".) For example, given the system of three equations below, organize them as follows:

$$\begin{array}{ll} (1) & a + 2b - c = 7 \\ (2) & 3a + c = 1 \\ (3) & -4a - b = -6 \end{array}$$

To solve a system of equations, use the elimination method. Although any number of equations can be added together at a time, it is usually more practical to only add two at a time. Next, add or subtract two equations so that the result is an equation that only contains the variables that appear in a third equation. For the example, add equations (1) and (2) in order to eliminate c, a variable which does not appear in equation (3):

$$\begin{array}{ll} (1) & a + 2b - c = 7 \\ (2) & \underline{3a + c = 1} \\ (4) & 4a + 2b = 8 \end{array}$$

Next add equations (3) and (4) to eliminate the variable a:

$$\begin{array}{ll} (3) & -4a - b = -6 \\ (4) & \underline{4a + 2b = 8} \\ & b = 2 \end{array}$$

Therefore, the solution for b is 2. Find the value of the other two variables by first substituting the value of b into equation (3) and solve the result for a. Then substitute the value of a into equation (2) and solve for c. The final solution is $a = 1$, $b = 2$, and $c = -2$. This general process can be used to solve systems of any number of equations and variables, but it becomes unwieldy very quickly as the number of equations and variables grow.

In addition, there are two other types of equations that are tested in this section: rational equations and radical equations. A rational equation is an equation in which some of the terms are fractions with a variable in their denominators. For instance, $x - \frac{6}{x-2} = 1$ is a rational equation because one term has $x - 2$ as its denominator. To solve a rational equation, eliminate the denominators by multiplying both sides of the equation by the denominator to cancel this value out.

For example, to solve $x - \frac{6}{x-2} = 1$, multiply both sides of by $(x - 2)$ and then simplify the result:

$$x - \frac{6}{x - 2} = 1$$
$$(x - 2)\left[x - \frac{6}{x - 2}\right] = (x - 2) \cdot 1$$
$$x(x - 2) - 6 = x - 2$$
$$x^2 - 2x - 6 = x - 2$$

Next solve the resulting equation for x:
$$x^2 - 3x - 4 = 0$$
$$(x + 1)(x - 4) = 0$$
$$x + 1 = 0 \quad \text{or} \quad x - 4 = 0$$
$$x = -1 \qquad\qquad x = 4$$

One thing that distinguishes rational equations from other types of equations is that some values of the variable result in division by zero. Therefore, when solving a rational equation, solutions must be checked to make sure that substituting them into the original equation does not cause division by zero. If so, they are not really solutions to the equation. In the example above, the original equation had $x - 2$ as one of its denominators. This expression is equal to zero only when $x = 2$, so the two solutions found, $x = -1$ and $x = 4$, do not cause division by zero and are valid solutions.

A radical equation has terms that are radicals and contain a variable. The equation $\sqrt{5x - 1} - 3 = 4$ is a radical equation because the radical $\sqrt{5x - 1}$ contains the variable x. Solve a radical equation by isolating the radical term and then squaring both sides of the equation to eliminate the radical. For example, to solve $\sqrt{5x - 1} - 3 = 4$, add 3 to both sides to isolate the radical term and then square both sides as follows:

$$\sqrt{5x - 1} - 3 = 4$$

$$\sqrt{5x - 1} = 7$$

$$(\sqrt{5x - 1})^2 = 49$$

$$5x - 1 = 49$$

Once the radical is removed, the equation can be solved for x:

$$5x = 50$$

$$x = 10$$

Note that when squaring both sides of an equation to find a solution for x, there is a risk of finding an incorrect solution. Substitute each solution into the original equation to determine if the solution is valid (produces a true equation.) For the example above, substitute the solution, $x = 10$, into the original equation:

$$\sqrt{5x - 1} - 3 = 4$$

$$\sqrt{5(10) - 1} - 3 = 4$$

$$\sqrt{49} - 3 = 4$$

$$7 - 3 = 4 \ \textit{True}$$

Since the result of the substitution is a true equality, the solution $x = 10$ is correct.

SOLUTIONS OF EQUATIONS AND INEQUALITIES QUESTIONS

1. If $4x^2 + 2x = 1$, then $x = ?$

    a. $-\dfrac{1}{8} \pm \dfrac{\sqrt{3}}{4}$

    b. $-\dfrac{1}{8} \pm \dfrac{\sqrt{5}}{4}$

    c. $-\dfrac{1}{4} \pm \dfrac{\sqrt{3}}{4}$

    d. $-\dfrac{1}{4} \pm \dfrac{\sqrt{5}}{4}$

2. Given $x^2 - 7x + 10 \geq 0$, what is the solution set for x?

    a. $2 \leq x \leq 5$
    b. $x \leq 2$ or $x \geq 5$
    c. $7 \leq x \leq 10$
    d. $x \leq 7$ or $x \geq 10$

3. If $x + 2y = 1$, $3y + z = 1$, and $-x + y + 3z = 8$, then $x = ?$

    a.   3
    b.   4
    c.   5
    d.   6

4. If $\dfrac{4}{x-3} - \dfrac{2}{x} = 1$, then $x = ?$

    a. -6
    b. -1
    c. -6 or -1
    d. -1 or 6

5. If $\sqrt{3x - 2} = x - 2$, then $x = ?$

    a.   1
    b.   6
    c. -1 or 6
    d.   1 or 6

Coordinate Geometry

This section measures the ability to solve problems involving coordinate geometry, or geometry involving the coordinate (or Cartesian) plane.

The coordinate plane relates geometric objects, like points and lines, to symbolic representations, like ordered pairs and equations. It is formed by the intersection of a horizontal number line (the x-axis) and a vertical number line (the y-axis) that meet at a point called the origin. These two axes divide the coordinate plane into four distinct regions called quadrants, which are labeled I, II, III, and IV as follows:

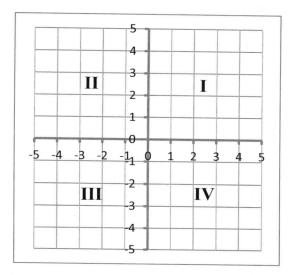

Based on the x- and y-axes, you can assign a unique pair of coordinates to every point in the plane. These coordinates are written as an ordered pair (x, y). The first number in the ordered pair, called the x-coordinate of the point, represents the point's distance to the left or right of the y-axis. If the x-coordinate is negative, then the point is to the left of the y-axis; if it is positive, then the point is to the right; if the value is zero then the point sits on the y-axis. The second number, called the y-coordinate of the point, represents the point's distance above or below the x-axis. If the y-coordinate is negative, then the point is below the x-axis; if it is positive, then the point is above the x-axis; if it is zero, then the point sits on the x-axis.

For instance, to graph (−2,4) on the coordinate grid, start at the origin and move 2 units to the left and then 4 units up. A dot on the grid at (-2,4) is used to represent this coordinate location graphically.

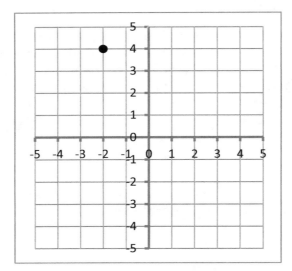

In addition to specific points, any equation can be graphed on the coordinate plane as long as it contains only the variables x and y. The graph of an equation is the set of points that satisfies the equation. If the graph of an equation is a line, then every point on that line represents a pair of values, x and y, that satisfies the original equation.

An equation can be graphed by substituting three or more values of x into the equation and then calculate the corresponding values of y. For convenience, these values can be organized into a table. For instance, to graph the equation $y = 2x - 3$, create a table of values like the one below:

x	$y = 2x - 3$	(x,y)
−1	$2(-1) - 3 = -5$	(−1,−5)
0	$2(0) - 3 = -3$	(0,−3)
1	$2(1) - 3 = -1$	(1,−1)

From the table, you can tell that the graph of this equation will pass through the points $(-1,-5)$, $(0,-3)$, and $(1,-1)$. Graph the equation by plotting these three points table and then connecting them with a straight line that extends infinitely in either direction:

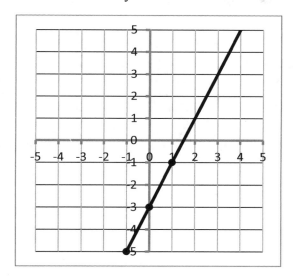

The graph of any linear equation is a straight line like the one above. Linear equations are often written in the form $y = mx + b$, which is called slope-intercept form because it can be used to easily determine the slope and y-intercept of the corresponding line. An equation in slope-intercept form $y = mx + b$ has a slope represented by the value m and a y-intercept represented by the value b.

The slope of a line is a measure of its steepness. A line that is nearly vertical has a very large slope (or a very small slope if it is negative), while a line that is horizontal or nearly horizontal has a slope that is closer to zero. If the line goes up as you go from left to right, then its slope is positive; if it goes down, the slope is negative. The slope can be calculated by choosing two points on the line, (x_1, y_1) and (x_2, y_2), and substituting the values of x_1, y_1, x_2, and y_2 into the equation $m = \frac{y_2 - y_1}{x_2 - x_1}$. In other words, compute the differences between the x- and y-coordinates and then divide the change in y by the change in x. For example, in the table of values above, the line $y = 2x - 3$ contains the points $(0,-3)$ and $(1,-1)$. Therefore, the slope of the line is $\frac{-1-(-3)}{1-0} = 2$, which confirms what the slope-intercept form of the equation also indicates, $m = 2$.

The relationship between the slopes of two lines can provide useful information about those lines. Two lines that have the same slope are parallel, that is they do not intersect no matter how far extended in either direction. The converse is also true: if two lines are parallel, then they must have the same slope. Two lines are perpendicular if and only if their slopes are negative reciprocals. For instance, if a given line has a slope of 3, then every line parallel to it also has a slope of 3 and every line perpendicular to it has a slope of $-\frac{1}{3}$.

The y-intercept of a line is the y-coordinate of the point where the line intercepts the y-axis. For instance, the graph of $y = 2x - 3$ intercepts the y-axis at the point $(0,-3)$. Therefore, its y-intercept is -3, which confirms what the slope-intercept form of the equation also indicates, $b = -3$. Although it doesn't come up very much, lines also have an x-intercept, which is defined as the x-coordinate of the point where the line intercepts the x-axis.

When an equation for a line is in slope-intercept form $y = mx + b$, the slope and y-intercept, which are given by the values of m and b, can be easily determined. Conversely, if given a slope and y-intercept of a line, the equation for that line can be determined by substituting these values back into the equation of the form $y = mx + b$.

While linear equations are always graphed as straight lines, the graph of a quadratic equation can be any one of the four conic sections. A conic section is a curve obtained by the intersection of a cone and a plane. In particular, the four conic sections are the circle, the ellipse, the parabola, and the hyperbola. The chart below gives a general equation for each of the four conic sections as well as an example of each.

Conic Section	Equation	Example
Circle	$(x - h)^2 + (y - k)^2 = r^2$	
Ellipse	$\dfrac{(x-h)^2}{a^2} + \dfrac{(y-k)^2}{b^2} = 1$	
Parabola	$(x - h)^2 = 4a(y - k)$	
Hyperbola	$\dfrac{(x-h)^2}{a^2} - \dfrac{(y-k)^2}{b^2} = 1$	

Students must be able to graph inequalities on a coordinate plane as well. The graph of an inequality will not be a point, line, or curve; it will be a region represented by a shaded area. Every point in this region represents a pair of values, x and y, that satisfy the original inequality.

To graph an inequality, first graph its boundary line or lines: change the inequality sign to an equal sign and graph the result. If the original inequality contains a < or >, graph it with a dotted (or dashed) line to indicate that the points on the line are not part of the solution set; if the original inequality contains a ≤ or ≥, graph it with a solid line to indicate that the points are part of the solution set. For example, to graph $y > x + 1$, first graph the equation $y = x + 1$ with a dashed line:

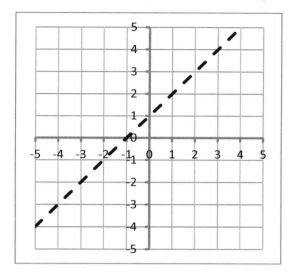

Next, shade the regions that are part of the solution set of the inequality. In the example above, shade either the region to the left of the dashed line or the region to the right of it. To choose which region to shade, choose test points in each of the regions. Then test these points by substituting their coordinates into the original inequality and simplifying the result. If the result is a true inequality, then the whole region that contains that test value should be shaded.

For the example above, test the point (0,0) (i.e. the origin) by substituting $x = 0$ and $y = 0$ into the original inequality:

$$y \geq x + 1$$

$$(0) \geq (0) + 1$$

$$0 \geq 1 \; false$$

Since the result is false, shade the other region of the graph, the region to the left of the line:

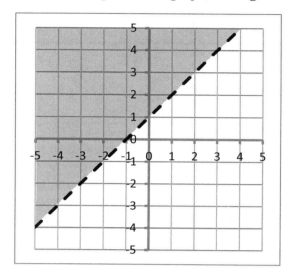

The resulting graph (including the shaded region, but not the dashed line), represents the solution set of the original inequality.

COORDINATE GEOMETRY QUESTIONS

1. What are the coordinates of vertices of the triangle below?

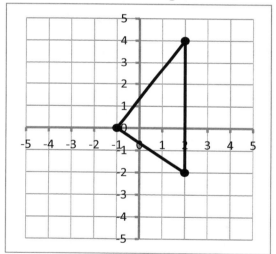

    a. (−1,0), (2,4), and (2,−2)
    b. (−1,0), (4,2), and (2,−2)
    c. (0,−1), (4,2), and (−2,2)
    d. (0,−1), (2,4), and (−2,2)

2. The equation of line L is $y = 3x + 4$. Which of the following is the equation of the line perpendicular to L that intersects at the point $(-3,-5)$?

    a. $y = -\dfrac{1}{3}x - 6$

    b. $y = -\dfrac{1}{3}x - 4$

    c. $y = \dfrac{1}{3}x - 6$

    d. $y = \dfrac{1}{3}x - 4$

3. What type of conic section does the equation $x^2 + y^2 = 11$ represent?

    a. Circle
    b. Ellipse
    c. Parabola
    d. Hyperbola

4. Which of the following graphs represents $y = x^2 + 2x - 1$?

a.
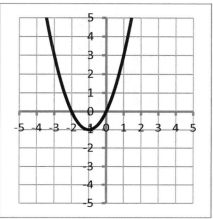

b.
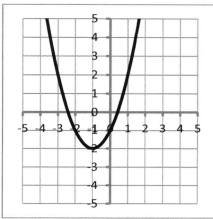

c.
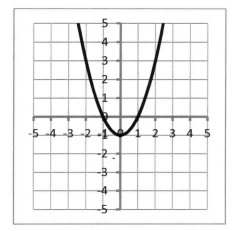

d.
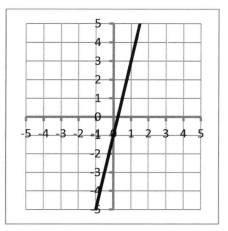

5. Which of the following graphs represents $y \leq 3x + 1$?

a.

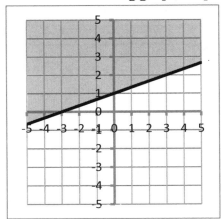

b.

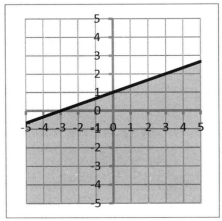

c.

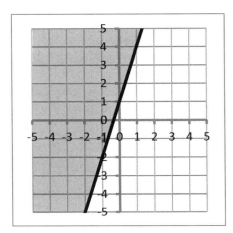

d.

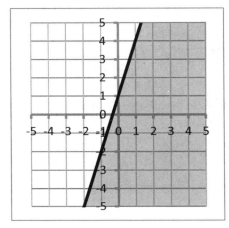

Applications and Other Algebra Topics

This section measures the ability to correctly solve problems involving advanced algebraic concepts such as complex numbers, sequences, permutations, and combinations. Some of the problems are word problems, therefore students must be able to interpret real-life situations while also applying these algebraic concepts correctly.

Based upon an understanding of the topics presented and the coordinate plane, equations like $x^2 + 1 = 0$ cannot be solved because any real number squared will always produce a positive number. However, in the 18th century, mathematicians started using a new number, represented by the letter i and defined as $\sqrt{-1}$, to solve equations such as this. Since $i = \sqrt{-1}$, it is also true that $i^2 = -1$. Therefore, the solutions of the equation $x^2 + 1 = 0$ are $x = i$ and $x = -i$.

Using the definition of i, the square root of any negative number can be rewritten as a real number times i. Numbers like this are called imaginary numbers. Some examples of imaginary numbers are $5i$, $\frac{3i}{2}$, and $2i\sqrt{5}$. Imaginary numbers are now universally accepted by mathematicians and have even found practical application in electrical engineering.

To simplify the square root of a negative number, rewrite it as the product of two radicals, $\sqrt{-1}$ and the square root of a positive number, and then simplify the result.

For example, $\sqrt{-27}$ can be simplified as follows:
$$\sqrt{-27} = \sqrt{-1} \times \sqrt{27}$$
$$= i \times 3\sqrt{3}$$
$$= 3i\sqrt{3}$$

The set of numbers that includes every real and imaginary number is the set of complex numbers. A complex number is any number that can be written in the form $a + bi$, where a and b are real numbers and i is the imaginary unit described above.

Complex numbers sometimes come up as solutions to quadratic equations. The quadratic formula (shown below), used to solve a quadratic equation in the form $ax^2 + bx + c = 0$, can demonstrate this:

$$x = \frac{-b \pm \sqrt{b^2 - 4ac}}{2a}$$

The quadratic formula contains a square root whose radicand is $b^2 - 4ac$. If this quantity (which is called the discriminant of the equation) is negative, the solution to the equation will be two complex numbers. In a more general sense, the discriminant of an equation can be used to determine the number and nature of the equation's solutions as follows:

1. If the discriminant is zero, then the equation has one real, rational solution.
2. If it is a positive perfect square, then the equation has two real, rational solutions.
3. If it is positive and not a perfect square, then the equation has two real, irrational solutions.
4. If it is negative, then the equation has two solutions that are complex conjugates (i.e. two complex numbers in the forms $a + bi$ and $a - bi$).

A sequence is a list of numbers. The numbers that make up the sequence are called its terms. For convenience, the notation a_1 is used for the first term of the sequence, the notation a_2 is used for the second term, and a_n represents the nth term of the sequence for any positive value of n. The terms of a sequence may be based on a pattern (i.e. a rule to get from one term to the next), or they may have no relationship to the other terms. In this section, two types of sequences that are infinitely long and based on simple rules will be covered.

An arithmetic sequence is a sequence in which each term is a specific constant more than the one before it. For instance, in the sequence below, each term can be found by adding -7 to the term before it:

$$16, 9, 2, -5, -12, -19, \ldots$$

The constant that must be added to each term to get the next one is called the common difference of the sequence and is represented by the variable d. In the example above, the common difference of the sequence is $d = -7$.

The nth term of an arithmetic sequence can be found by writing out each term of the sequence until reaching the nth term, however this can be very time consuming. A much easier way is to use the formula for the nth term of an arithmetic sequence:

$$a_n = a_1 + (n - 1)d$$

For example, to calculate the 40th term of the sequence above, substitute the values $n = 40$, $a_1 = 16$, and $d = -7$ into this formula and simplify the result:

$$a_{40} = 16 + (40 - 1) \cdot (-7)$$

$$= 16 + 39 \cdot (-7)$$

$$= -257$$

There is a method to calculate the sum of the first n terms of an arithmetic sequence, which is written as S_n. First calculate the sum of the first nine terms of the sequence above by writing out the terms explicitly:

$$S_9 = 16 + 9 + 2 + (-5) + (-12) + (-19) + (-26) + (-33) + (-40)$$

Note that specific pairs of terms add up to the same number: the first and last terms of the sequence add up to -24, the second and second-to-last terms add up to -24, and so on as shown below:

The sum of a_1 and a_9 is $16 + (-40) = -24$.

The sum of a_2 and a_8 is $9 + (-33) = -24$.

The sum of a_3 and a_7 is $2 + (-26) = -24$.

The sum of a_4 and a_6 is $(-5) + (-19) = -24$.

The one term not paired is $a_6 = -12$, which is exactly half of -24. Thus, the sum of the first nine terms of the sequence is $4\frac{1}{2}$ (or $\frac{9}{2}$) times the sum of a_1 and a_9:

$$S_9 = \frac{9}{2}[16 + (-40)]$$

$$= \frac{9}{2}(-24)$$

$$= -108$$

The sum of the first n terms of an arithmetic sequence as demonstrated above can be generalized to provide a formula for S_n:

$$S_n = \frac{n}{2}(a_1 + a_n)$$

A second type of sequence that is tested in this section is called a geometric sequence. A geometric sequence is a sequence in which each term is a specific constant times the term before it. For example, in the sequence below, each term can be found by multiplying the preceding term by 3:

$$\frac{2}{9}, \frac{2}{3}, 2, 6, 18, 54, \dots$$

The constant that is multiplied with each term in a geometric sequence is called the common ratio of the sequence and is represented by the variable r. In the example above, the common ratio of the sequence is $r = 3$.

In addition, there are two formulas used to find specific values related to a given geometric sequence. The nth term of a geometric sequence can be found using the formula for a_n:

$$a_n = a_1 r^{n-1}$$

The sum of the first n terms of a geometric sequence can be found using the formula for S_n:

$$S_n = \frac{a_1(1-r^n)}{1-r}$$

The last topic in this section involves interpreting and solving word problems using permutations and combinations. A permutation is an arrangement of a set of objects in which the order of the objects does matter. For example, the first three letters of the alphabet can be combined into six distinct two-letter permutations as follows:

AB   AC   BA   BC   CA   CB

The notation $_nP_k$ gives the number of different permutations possible with a total of n objects to form a group of k objects without using an object more than once. The value of $_nP_k$ can be found using the formula below:

$$_nP_k = \frac{n!}{(n-k)!}$$

The exclamation mark (!) is the symbol for the factorial of a number. The factorial of a number is defined as the product of all the whole numbers less than or equal to it. The value of 7! is:

$$7! = 7 \times 6 \times 5 \times 4 \times 3 \times 2 \times 1$$

$$= 5040$$

On the other hand, a combination is an arrangement of a set of objects in which the order of the objects does not matter. For example, the first four letters of the alphabet can be arranged into four

59

distinct three-letter combinations if letters are not used more than once. Since order does not matter, ABC and BAC are counted as the same combination:

ABC   ABD   ACD   BCD

The notation $\binom{n}{k}$ gives the number of different combinations possible among a total of n objects to form a group of k objects without using an object more than once. The value of $\binom{n}{k}$ can be found using the formula below:

$$\binom{n}{k} = \frac{n!}{k!(n-k)!}$$

APPLICATIONS AND OTHER ALGEBRA TOPICS QUESTIONS

1. If $2x(x + 1) = -3$, then $x = ?$

   a. $-\frac{1}{2} \pm \frac{\sqrt{5}}{2}$

   b. $-\frac{1}{2} \pm \frac{\sqrt{7}}{2}$

   c. $-\frac{1}{2} \pm \frac{i\sqrt{5}}{2}$

   d. $-\frac{1}{2} \pm \frac{i\sqrt{7}}{2}$

2. What is the sum of the first 20 terms of the sequence 2, 5, 8, 11, …?

   a.   59
   b.   61
   c.   590
   d.   610

3. There are 500 bacteria in a Petri dish. If the number of bacteria doubles every day, how many bacteria will be in the Petri dish in 14 days?

   a.   102,400
   b.   204,800
   c.   306,800
   d.   409,600

4. A committee of 12 people is electing four of its members for president, vice president, secretary, and treasurer. In how many different ways can they elect these four positions?

   a.   1680
   b.   9240
   c.   11,880
   d.   20,736

5. Using a standard deck, how many different five-card hands consist only of spades?

   a.   1287
   b.   6435
   c.   51,480
   d.   154,440

Functions and Trigonometry

This section measures the ability to correctly solve problems involving various types of functions and their properties. Functions are mathematical objects that return an output value for every valid input put into them. Functions assign exactly one output value to each input.

Functions are written in a notation called function notation. In function notation, $f(x)$ (read "f of x") represents a function called f whose input value is x. As an example, if the function f is defined as $(x) = x^2 + 5x$, then its output is the value of the expression $x^2 + 5x$ for any particular x-value in its domain. To calculate $f(x)$ for a specific value of x, substitute that value into $x^2 + 5x$ and then simplify the result:

$$f(-3) = (-3)^2 + 5(-3)$$

$$= 9 - 15$$

$$= -6$$

The set of all possible input values that can be evaluated by a function is called the function's domain. Many functions can take any real numbers as an input value, so their domain is the set of all real numbers. Some examples of functions like this are shown below:

$$f(x) = 6x^2 + 3x - 4 \qquad g(x) = 3^x \qquad h(x) = \sqrt[3]{2x - 7} + 1$$

Other functions are only defined for a specific subset of all real numbers. One way to find the domain of a function is to look at all the different operations that are used in the function and determine if one or more of them is undefined for some values of the input. Then the domain of the function will be the set of all real numbers except those input values. For example, division by zero is undefined. Therefore, the domain of the function $f(x) = \frac{2}{x-1}$ is all real numbers except $x = 1$ which would cause division by zero. This particular domain is also sometimes written as $x \neq 1$.

Another way to find the domain of a function is to graph it on a coordinate plane. The domain of $f(x) = \sqrt{x}$ can be found by graphing the equation $= \sqrt{x}$. The domain of the f is the set of all x-values that the graph is defined for.

The set of all possible output values of the function is called the function's range. The range of a function can be found by graphing it on a coordinate plane. In the graph, the range of the function is the set of all y-values that the graph is defined for.

The inverse of a function is a function that undoes the original function. The inverse of $f(x) = 2x$ is $g(x) = \frac{x}{2}$ because, for any value of x, if $f(x) = y$, then $g(y) = x$. The inverse of $f(x)$ is notated as $f^{-1}(x)$, such as $f^{-1}(x) = \frac{x}{2}$. Many inverse functions can be determined intuitively; the inverse of "multiplying a number by 2" is "dividing a number by 2", therefore the inverse of $f(x) = 2x$ is $f^{-1}(x) = \frac{x}{2}$.

The inverse of a more complex functions, like $h(x) = \frac{3}{2x} + 7$, may not be as intuitive to find. In this case, start with the definition of $h(x)$ and then replace $h(x)$ with y:

$$h(x) = \frac{3}{2x} + 7$$

$$y = \frac{3}{2x} + 7$$

Next switch all the x's and y's and solve for y:

$$x = \frac{3}{2y} + 7$$

$$x - 7 = \frac{3}{2y}$$

$$2y(x - 7) = 3$$

$$2y = \frac{3}{x-7}$$

$$y = \frac{3}{2(x-7)}$$

Finally, replace y with $h^{-1}(x)$ to notate the inverse of the original function:

$$h^{-1}(x) = \frac{3}{2(x-7)}$$

The composition of two functions is a function formed by combining the two functions so that the output of one is the input of the other. The notation for the composition of two functions, $f(x)$ and $g(x)$, is $(f \circ g)(x)$, which is defined by the equation $(f \circ g)(x) = (f(g(x))$. To find the composition of two functions, substitute the output of the second function for the input of the first function and then simplify the result. For instance, if the functions f and g are defined as $f(x) = 3x + 1$ and $g(x) = 2x^2$, then the composition is:

$$(f \circ g)(x) = f(2x^2)$$

$$= 3(2x^2) + 1$$

$$= 6x^2 + 1$$

The problems in this section contain five different types of functions: polynomial, rational, exponential, logarithmic, and trigonometric functions. Students must be able to evaluate each of these types of functions for specific input values, identify the domain and range, find the inverse, and calculate the composition of two functions.

A polynomial function is a function that contains a polynomial. The function $f(x) = x^4 - \frac{1}{2}x + 3$ is an example of a polynomial function. The terms of a polynomial function are usually written in descending order of exponents. Thus, the expression below is the general form for a polynomial function, in which the a's are constants and n is the largest exponent in the polynomial (i.e. the degree of the polynomial):

$$f(x) = a_n x^n + a_{n-1} x^{n-1} + \cdots + a_2 x^2 + a_1 x + a_0$$

An exponential function is a function in which the input variable is an exponent of a constant. The general form for an exponential function is $f(x) = a^x$, where a is a constant. An exponential function is not the same as a function in the form $f(x) = x^a$. Besides having different output values, the two also have different types of inverses. Whereas the inverse of a function like $f(x) = x^3$ is a radical function (a function containing a root of the input), in this case the cube root of x, the inverse of an exponential function is a logarithmic function (a function containing the logarithm of the input.)

The logarithm of a number x is the exponent that another number b must be raised to in order to get that number. The number b is called the base of the logarithm. Logarithms are notated as $\log_b x$ (read "the logarithm of x to base b"). For example, since $10^3 = 1000$, the value of $\log_{10} 1000$ is 3.

Trigonometric functions are functions of an angle that are based on the proportions of a right triangle. The input value for the functions, an angle, is usually represented by the Greek letter θ ("theta.") The three main trigonometric functions are sine, cosine, and tangent. They are defined as the ratios of the sides of a right triangle:

$$sin\ \theta = \frac{\text{opposite}}{\text{hypotenuse}} \qquad cos\ \theta = \frac{\text{adjacent}}{\text{hypotenuse}} \qquad tan\ \theta = \frac{\text{opposite}}{\text{adjacent}}$$

For example, in the right triangle below, the side opposite θ is 3 units long, the side adjacent to θ is 4 units long, and the hypotenuse of the triangle (the longest side) is 5 units long. Therefore, the values of trigonometric functions for the angle θ are $\theta = \frac{3}{5}$, $cos\ \theta = \frac{4}{5}$, and $tan\ \theta = \frac{3}{4}$.

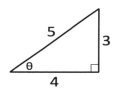

The mnemonic SOH-CAH-TOA can be used to help remember the definitions of the three trigonometric functions. SOH-CAH-TOA stands for "Sine = Opposite ÷ Hypotenuse, Cosine = Adjacent ÷ Hypotenuse, Tangent = Opposite ÷ Adjacent."

FUNCTIONS AND TRIGONOMETRY QUESTIONS

1. If $f(x) = 4x^3 + 5x^2 - 2$, then $f\left(-\frac{1}{2}\right) = ?$

    a. $-\frac{13}{2}$

    b. $-\frac{15}{4}$

    c. $-\frac{5}{4}$

    d. $-\frac{1}{4}$

2. What is the domain of $(x) = \frac{4}{x+2}$?

    a. $x \neq -2$

    b. $x < 4$

    c. $x \geq 2$

    d.   All Real Numbers

3. If $f(x) = 2x - 4$ and $g(x) = \frac{3x+1}{2}$, then $(f \circ g)(x) = ?$

   a. $3x - \frac{11}{2}$

   b. $3x - 3$

   c. $6x - \frac{11}{2}$

   d. $6x - 3$

4. If $h(x) = \log_{10}(x + 2)$, then $h^{-1}(x) = ?$

   a. 10^{x-2}

   b. 10^{x+2}

   c. $10^x - 2$

   d. $10^x + 2$

5. If θ is an acute angle and $\sin \theta = \frac{5}{7}$, then $\cos \theta = ?$

   a. $\frac{2}{7}$

   b. $\frac{2}{5}$

   c. $\frac{4}{7}$

   d. $\frac{2\sqrt{6}}{7}$

Answers and Explanations

Arithmetic

COMPUTATIONS WITH INTEGERS AND FRACTIONS

1. A: According to the order of operations (PEMDAS), first subtract to find the value in the parentheses, then multiply the result by 5, and finally divide by 3:

$$5(3 - 9) \div 3 = 5(-6) \div 3$$
$$= -30 \div 3$$
$$= -10$$

2. B: According to the order of operations (PEMDAS), first simplify the numerator and the denominator of the expression, then perform the division:

$$\frac{4 - (-12)}{-9 + 5} = \frac{4 + 12}{-9 + 5}$$
$$\frac{16}{-4}$$
$$= -4$$

3. A: According to the order of operations (PEMDAS), start with the expression in parentheses. To add two fractions, rewrite them with a common denominator and then add the numerators. Keep in mind that the first fraction is negative and the second is positive:

$$4\left(-\frac{1}{2} + \frac{3}{5}\right) = 4\left(\frac{-5}{10} + \frac{6}{10}\right)$$
$$= 4\left(\frac{1}{10}\right)$$

Next multiply the result by 4 and simplify the result by putting it in lowest terms:

$$4\left(\frac{1}{10}\right) = \frac{4}{10}$$
$$= \frac{2}{5}$$

4. B: First rewrite the fractions with a common denominator. The lowest common denominator (LCD) of the denominators (15, 20, 5, and 30) is 60. Multiply the numerator and denominator of the each fraction to make their denominators 60:

$$\frac{7}{15}, \frac{9}{20}, \frac{2}{5}, \frac{13}{30} \rightarrow \frac{28}{60}, \frac{27}{60}, \frac{24}{60}, \frac{26}{60}$$

Then put the new list in order from least to greatest by comparing numerators:

$$\frac{28}{60}, \frac{27}{60}, \frac{24}{60}, \frac{26}{60} \rightarrow \frac{24}{60}, \frac{26}{60}, \frac{27}{60}, \frac{28}{60}$$

65

Finally, change the fractions back to their original forms:

$$\frac{24}{60}, \frac{26}{60}, \frac{27}{60}, \frac{28}{60} \rightarrow \frac{2}{5}, \frac{13}{30}, \frac{9}{20}, \frac{7}{15}$$

5. C: To divide two fractions, invert the second fraction by switching its numerator and denominator:

$$\frac{3}{8} \div \frac{6}{11} = \frac{3}{8} \times \frac{11}{6}$$

Next perform the multiplication to get the answer. Before multiplying the two fractions, cancel any common factors that appear in the numerator of one fraction and the denominator of another to ensure the result is in lowest terms. Here, cancel 3 from the numerator of the first fraction and the denominator of the second:

$$\frac{3}{8} \times \frac{11}{6} = \frac{1}{8} \times \frac{11}{2}$$

Last, multiply the fractions. Multiply the numerators and the denominators separately, and put the products into a new fraction:

$$\frac{1}{8} \times \frac{11}{2} = \frac{11}{16}$$

COMPUTATION WITH DECIMAL NUMBERS

1. C: The easiest way to add three numbers is to set up the addition vertically. Line up the decimal points of the three numbers and add, bringing down the decimal point:

$$\begin{array}{r} 8.31 \\ 6.7 \\ +1.889 \\ \hline 16.899 \end{array}$$

2. B: The easiest way to multiply two numbers is to set up the multiplication vertically. Start by multiplying the numbers normally as if they were whole numbers:

$$\begin{array}{r} 12.94 \\ \times\ \ 5.8 \\ \hline 10352 \\ +\ 64700 \\ \hline 75052 \end{array}$$

Next you need to decide where to put the decimal point in the answer. In the original numbers, 12.94 and 5.8, the first number has two digits after the decimal point, and the second has just one. Therefore, you should place the decimal point three places from the rightmost digit of the product. The correct answer is 75.052.

3. A: The tenths place is the first digit after the decimal. In this case, it is a 5. To round to the nearest tenth, the given number will either be rounded down to 94.5 or rounded up to 94.6. To determine which way to round, look at the digit after the 5 (the hundredths place), which is a 4. Since this number is less than five, round down. Therefore, the correct answer is 94.5.

4. C: Since the problem involves multiplying three quantities together, you could multiply from left-to-right. However, a much easier way to solve the problem is to realize that one of the quantities is zero. The product of zero and any other number is zero, thus the answer must be zero.

5. A: The easiest way to subtract two decimals is to set up the subtraction vertically. Rewrite each number so that they all have the same number of digits after the decimal. Then subtract vertically:

$$14.320$$
$$- 12.915$$
$$1.405$$

PROBLEMS INVOLVING PERCENTS

1. D: First convert the percent to a decimal number by dividing it by 100, or, equivalently, by moving the decimal point two places to the left:

$$56\% = 0.56$$

Next, calculate 56% of 25 by multiplying 25 by 0.56:

$$0.56 \times 25 = 14$$

2. B: A percent can be converted to a fraction by putting it over 100, then reducing to lowest terms by finding the greatest common factor (GCF) of the numerator and denominator:

$$45\% = \frac{45}{100} = \frac{9}{20}$$

3. C: A percent is a part divided by the whole ($\frac{part}{whole}$). In this problem, the part is 42 and the whole is 56, so the percent can be expressed as $\frac{42}{56}$, or .075:

$$\frac{42}{56} = 42 \div 56$$

$$= 0.75$$

Convert the decimal to a percent by multiplying it by 100 (or equivalently by moving the decimal point two places to the right) and adding a percent sign:

$$0.75 = 75\%$$

4. C: First add the numbers of boys and girls to find the total number of students:

$$48 + 72 = 120$$

Use this total to find the percent of the students that are boys. You can think of percents as a part divided by the whole ($\frac{part}{whole}$). The part is the number of boys, 48, and the whole is the total number of students, 120. Next convert the fraction $\frac{48}{120}$ to a decimal. Divide the numerator by the denominator to get a decimal number:

$$\frac{48}{120} = 48 \div 120$$

$$= 0.4$$

Last, convert the decimal to a percent by multiplying it by 100 (or equivalently by moving the decimal point two places to the right) and adding a percent sign:

$$0.4 = 40\%$$

5. A: Since the percent is given as a fraction, the first step will be to convert it to a decimal (but one that is still a percent):

$$\frac{1}{2}\% = 0.5\%$$

Convert the percent to a proper decimal number by dividing it by 100, or, equivalently, by moving the decimal point two places to the left:

$$0.5\% = 0.005$$

Finally, calculate 0.5% of 40 by multiplying 40 by 0.005:

$$0.005 \times 40 = 0.2$$

ESTIMATION, ORDERING, NUMBER SENSE

1. C: A perfect square is a positive integer that can be written as the square of another number. For instance, 16 and 100 are both perfect squares since $4^2 = 16$ and $10^2 = 100$. This problem asks for an estimate of the square root. The answer choice that when squared is closest to 82 is 9 since $9^2 = 81$.

2. D: To begin, round each number to its first decimal place:

$$80{,}389 \times 597.39 \approx 80{,}000 \times 600$$

Now multiply the rounded numbers. Multiplying numbers with a lot of zeroes can be done quickly even if the numbers are very large. First multiply the numbers without the zeroes:

$$8 \times 6 = 48$$

Next, add the zeroes that were removed. Since 80,000 has four zeroes and 600 has two, add six zeroes to the right side (4 + 2 = 6) to obtain the final result:

$$80{,}000 \times 600 = 48{,}000{,}000$$

3. A: Since the numbers provided are a fraction and three decimal numbers, it will be easier to compare these numbers by converting the fraction to a decimal:

$$\frac{8}{5} = 8 \div 5$$

$$= 1.6$$

The list now consists of 1.71, 1.6, −2, and 1.685. Since −2 is negative and the other numbers are positive, −2 must be the smallest of the four.

The remaining numbers are 1.71, 1.6 and 1.685 (or 1.710, 1.600, and 1.685). They all have a 1 in the ones place, so the ones place is inconclusive. Comparing the digits in the tenths place shows that 1.6 and 1.685 are both smaller than 1.71. Finally, comparing the hundredths place shows that 1.6 (or 1.600) is smaller than 1.695. Therefore, from least to greatest, the order of the numbers is as follows:

$$-2, 1.6, 1.685, 1.71 \quad \text{or} \quad -2, \tfrac{8}{5}, 1.685, 1.71$$

4. C: Since 47 is just a little more than 45, the first fraction, $\frac{47}{45}$, is a little more than 1. Similarly, 20 is a little less than 21, the second fraction, $\frac{20}{21}$, is a little less than 1. Therefore, when you add them up, the result will be very close to 2.

5. D: The greatest number is found by estimating each answer choice.

A) In choice A, the percent is about 25%, which is equal to one-fourth. One-fourth of 120 is 30. So, 24.1% of 120 is about 30.

B) In choice B, the second number is close to 100. If you take any percent of 100, the result is the original percent. For instance, 81% of 100 is equal to 81. Therefore, 34.2% of 99 is about 34.

C) In choice C, the percent is about 50%, which is equal to one-half. One-half of 72 is 36. So, 49.4% of 72 is about 36.

D) In choice D, the percent is also about 50. One-half of 90 is 45. So, 51.1% of 90 is about 45.

Since 45 is much larger than the other estimations, the best answer is choice D.

WORD PROBLEMS AND APPLICATIONS

1. C: The problem states that three-fifths of the 300 students are girls, so calculate the product of three-fifths $(\tfrac{3}{5})$ and 300:

$$\frac{3}{5} \cdot an = \frac{3}{5} \cdot \frac{300}{1}$$
$$= \frac{3}{1} \cdot \frac{60}{1}$$
$$= 180$$

2. A: First add the cost of the three items together:

$$\begin{array}{r} 2.55 \\ 3.79 \\ +\,3.09 \\ \hline 9.43 \end{array}$$

Subtract this amount from $20.00 to find the change:

$$\begin{array}{r} 20.00 \\ -\,9.43 \\ \hline \end{array}$$

10.57

3. A: First calculate the dollar value of the sales tax. To find this value, multiply $25,000 by 0.05:

$$0.05 \cdot \$25,000 = \$1,250$$

To find the total cost of the car with sales tax, add the sales tax to the original price of the car:

$$\$25,000 + \$1,250 = \$26,250$$

4. B: First add the number of boys and girls to find the total number of students in the school:

$$270 + 450 = 720$$

Next, divide the number of boys, 270, by 720 and convert the result to a percent:

$$270 \div 720 = 0.375$$

$$= 37.5\%$$

5. D: Find the total revenue by multiplying the number of computers by the price of each computer. Since the question uses the word "approximately", estimate this amount by first rounding the numbers:

$$810,602 \approx 800,000$$

$$\$895 \approx \$900$$

Then multiply the rounded numbers:

$$800,000 \cdot \$900 = \$720,000,000$$

Therefore, the total revenue was about $720 million.

Elementary Algebra

REAL NUMBERS

1. D: The set of real numbers is comprised of two main types of numbers: rational numbers and irrational numbers. A rational number is a number that can be written as a fraction. Integers, fractions, and repeating or terminating decimal numbers are all rational numbers since they can all be written as fractions. Irrational numbers, on the other hand, are numbers that cannot be written as fractions.

Look at the given choices starting with choice A and determine one which is irrational. Choice A is a rational number since $-5 = -\frac{5}{1}$. Choice B is given in fractional form already so it is rational as well. Choice C is a repeating decimal equal to $\frac{1}{3}$ so it is rational. Choice D, however, is π (the Greek letter "pi"), the symbol for a specific decimal number (approximately 3.1416) that goes on forever without repeating. Thus, it is the only irrational number among the choices.

2. C: First simplify the expression in parentheses. To subtract two fractions, rewrite them with a common denominator and then subtract the numerators:

$$\left(\frac{2}{3} - \frac{1}{4}\right) \div \frac{1}{4} = \left(\frac{8}{12} - \frac{3}{12}\right) \div \frac{1}{4}$$

$$= \frac{5}{12} \div \frac{1}{4}$$

Now divide the fractions. Invert the second fraction by switching its numerator and denominator and change the operation to multiplication. Cancel any common factors that appear in the numerator of one fraction and the denominator of another to simplify the multiplication:

$$\frac{5}{12} \div \frac{1}{4} = \frac{5}{12} \times \frac{4}{1}$$

$$= \frac{5}{3} \times \frac{1}{1}$$

$$= \frac{5}{3}$$

3. C: First simplify the numerator and the denominator:

$$\frac{4.8 - 12.3}{-1 - 4} = \frac{-7.5}{-5}$$

Next, simplify the resulting fraction by dividing:

$$\frac{-7.5}{-5} = -7.5 \div (-5)$$

$$= 1.5$$

4. A: Evaluate a square root by first factoring the radicand (the number under the radical sign) by taking out the greatest perfect square that divides it evenly. In this problem, the radicand is 63, whose greatest perfect square factor is 9. Next rewrite the result as the product of two radicals:

$$\sqrt{63} = \sqrt{9 \times 7}$$

$$= \sqrt{9} \times \sqrt{7}$$

Finally, finish simplifying the result using the fact that $\sqrt{9} = 3$:

$$\sqrt{9} \times \sqrt{7} = 3\sqrt{7}$$

5. B: Multiply square root radicals by multiplying the radicands (the numbers under the radical sign) and putting the result under a square root sign:

$$\sqrt{3} \times \sqrt{7} = \sqrt{3 \times 7}$$

$$= \sqrt{21}$$

Linear Equations, Inequalities and Systems

1. A: First simplify the left side of the equation by distributing the −4 and then adding the constants together:

$$2 - 4(x + 3) = 6$$

$$2 - 4x - 12 = 6$$

$$-4x - 10 = 6$$

Next isolate the variable x by adding 10 to both sides. Last, divide both sides by the coefficient of x, −4, to solve the equation:

$$-4x = 16$$

$$x = -4$$

2. B: First simplify the right side of the equation by combining like terms:

$$3a = 2a + a + 4a - 4$$

$$3a = 7a - 4$$

Next, subtract $3a$ and add 4 to both sides of the equation to isolate the variable on the right side. Finally, solve the resulting equation by dividing both sides by the coefficient of a, 4:

$$3a = 7a - 4$$

$$0 = 4a - 4$$

$$4 = 4a$$

$$1 = a$$

3. B: Inequalities are solved in much the same way as equations. The only difference is that if multiplying or dividing both sides by a negative number, the inequality sign must be flipped (i.e. > becomes <, ≥ becomes ≤.) Begin by isolating the variable y by subtracting 4 from both sides:

$$4 - \frac{1}{3}y > 5$$

$$-\frac{1}{3}y > 1$$

Then solve the resulting inequality by multiplying both sides by −3 to get rid of the coefficient of y. Since this involves multiplying both sides of the inequality by a negative number, flip the inequality sign as well:

$$y < -3$$

4. A: The given equations form a system of linear equations. Since one equation has x and the other has $-x$, the elimination method is a good choice. First add the equations together to eliminate the variable x:

$$\begin{aligned} x + 3y &= 3 \\ \underline{-x + y} &= \underline{5} \\ 4y &= 8 \end{aligned}$$

Then solve the resulting equation for y by dividing both sides by 4:

$$y = 2$$

Finally, to calculate the value of x, substitute 2 for y into one of the equations and solve for x:

$$x + 3(2) = 3$$

$$x + 6 = 3$$

$$x = -3$$

5. C: The given equations form a system of linear equations. Since the first equation is already given in terms of x, it will be easier to solve it using the substitution method. Start by substituting $2y - 3$ for x in the second equation:

$$2x + \frac{1}{2}y = 3$$

$$2(2y - 3) + \frac{1}{2}y = 3$$

Next, solve the resulting equation for y. Distribute the 2 and then combine like y-terms in the result:

$$4y - 6 + \frac{1}{2}y = 3$$

$$\frac{9}{2}y - 6 = 3$$

Finally, isolate the variable y by adding 6 to both sides and then dividing both sides by the coefficient of y, which is $\frac{9}{2}$ (or, equivalently, multiply by 2 and divide by 9):

$$\frac{9}{2}y = 9$$

$$y = 2$$

QUADRATIC EXPRESSIONS AND EQUATIONS

1. A: To add quadratic expressions, combine like terms. In this problem, there are three sets of like terms: the y^2-terms, the y-terms, and the constants. Set up the addition vertically, making sure to line up like terms, and then add them together:

$$
\begin{aligned}
& y^2 + 9y - 2 \\
+\ & 4y^2 - y - 5 \\
\hline
& 5y^2 + 8y - 7
\end{aligned}
$$

2. D: To multiply two binomials, use FOIL. FOIL is an acronym that stands for "First, Outer, Inner, Last." Multiply the first terms of the binomial, then the outer terms of the binomials, then the inner terms of the binomials, and finally the last terms of the binomials:

Multiply the First terms of $(\boldsymbol{x} + 3)(\boldsymbol{x} - 1)$: $x \cdot x = x^2$

Multiply the Outer terms of $(\boldsymbol{x} + 3)(x - \boldsymbol{1})$: $x \cdot (-1) = -x$

Multiply the Inner terms of $(x + \boldsymbol{3})(\boldsymbol{x} - 1)$: $3 \cdot x = 3x$

Multiply the Last terms of $(x + \boldsymbol{3})(x - \boldsymbol{1})$: $3 \cdot (-1) = -3$

Next, add the products and simplify the result by combining like terms:

$$(x + 3)(x - 1) = x^2 - x + 3x - 3$$

$$= x^2 + 2x - 3$$

3. D: Simplify the expression by pulling out the greatest common factor between the two terms, which is 2:

$$2c^2 - 32 = 2(c^2 - 16)$$

Next, factor the expression in parentheses. Since c^2 is the square of c and 16 is the square of 4, $c^2 - 16$ is the difference of two squares. Therefore, it can be factored as $a^2 - b^2 = (a - b)(a + b)$. For this problem, use the values $a = c$ and $b = 4$:

$$2(c^2 - 16 = 2(c - 4)(c + 4)$$

4. B: The given equation is a quadratic equation that can be solved by factorization. First, move everything to one side to get it in the correct form, by subtracting 6 from both sides:

$$x^2 + 5x = 6$$

$$x^2 + 5x - 6 = 0$$

Since the left side expression is a trinomial in the form $ax^2 + bx + c$ with $a = 1$, the factorization will be a product of two binomials in the form $(x + a)(x + b)$. The values of a and b are two numbers that add up to 5 and have a product of -6. The only numbers that satisfy these requirements are 1 and -6. Substitute these values into $(x + a)(x + b)$ to get the factorization of the trinomial:

$$x^2 + 5x - 6 = 0$$

$$(x - 1)(x + 6) = 0$$

Finally, use the zero-product rule to solve for x. The zero-product rule states that if the product of two expressions is zero, then one of the expressions must be zero. For this problem that means that either $x + 1$ is zero or $x - 6$ is zero. Set each factor to zero and solve for x:

$$x - 1 = 0 \quad \text{or} \quad x + 6 = 0$$

$$x = 1 \qquad\qquad x = -6$$

Therefore, the solutions to the equation are $x = 1$ and $x = -6$.

5. B: The given equation is a quadratic equation that can be solved by factoring. Since it is a trinomial in the form $ax^2 + bx + c$ with $a > 1$, the factorization will be a product of two binomials in the form $(ax + b)(cx + d)$. Use trial-and-error to find the correct values of a, b, c, and d. In this case, the values of a and c must multiply to 2 (the coefficient of the n^2-term), so they must be 1 and 2; the values of b and d must multiply to 4 (the coefficient), so they can either be 1 and 4 or 2 and 2. Try different combinations until finding the correct n-term. For instance, the following combination does not work because the n-term comes out to $6n$, instead of $9n$:

$$(n + 1)(2n + 4) = 2n^2 + 4n + 2n + 4$$

$$= 2n^2 + 6n + 4$$

The following is the correct factorization:

$$2n^2 + 9n + 4 = 0$$

$$(n + 4)(2n + 1) = 0$$

Next solve for n by using the zero-product rule. The zero-product rule states that if the product of two expressions is zero, then one of the expressions must be zero. For this problem that means that either $2n + 1$ is zero or $n + 4$ is zero. Set each factor to zero and solve for n:

$$n + 4 = 0 \quad \text{or} \quad 2n + 1 = 0$$

$$n = -4 \qquad\qquad n = -\frac{1}{2}$$

Therefore, the solutions to the equation are $n = -4$ and $= -\frac{1}{2}$.

ALGEBRAIC EXPRESSIONS AND EQUATIONS

1. B: To evaluate the expression for the given values of x and y, substitute the values into the expression and then calculate the result:

$$2x^2 + 5x - y^2 = 2(3)^2 + 5(3) - (5)^2$$

$$= 2 \cdot 9 + 5 \cdot 3 - 25$$

$$= 18 + 15 - 25$$

$$= 8$$

2. B: A solution satisfies an equation if it makes the equation true. Substitute each x-value into the equation to see if the result is a true equality. Start with choice A, $x = 2$:

$$5x = 15$$

$$5(2) = 15$$

$$10 = 15$$

Since the resulting equation is false, $x = 2$ does not satisfy the given equation. Next try choice B, $x = 3$:

$$5x = 15$$

$$5(3) = 15$$

$$15 = 15$$

Since the resulting equation is true, $x = 3$ satisfies the given equation.

3. B: To divide expressions that contain variables, divide pairs of like variables (or constants) that appear in both the numerator and denominator. For this problem, first divide the constants: $12 \div 3$, then divide the a's: $a^2 \div a$. Since $a^2 \div a$ is equivalent to $\frac{a^2}{a^1}$, use the quotient rule, $\frac{x^a}{x^b} = x^{a-b}$, to simplify it. There is no change to b since the divisor does not contain the variable b:

$$\frac{12a^2b}{3a} = \frac{4a^{2-1}b}{1}$$

$$= 4ab$$

4. D: The quickest method to evaluate this expression is to distribute the exponent of 2 to each of the values inside the parenthesis using the rule $(x^a)^b = x^{a \cdot b}$:

$$(4x^5)^2 = 4^2 \cdot x^{5 \cdot 2}$$

$$= 16x^{10}$$

5. A: To simplify the given expression, start by distributing the 3 across $(2y - x)$:

$$4x + 3(2y - x) = 4x + 3 \cdot 2y + 3 \cdot (-x)$$

$$= 4x + 6y - 3x$$

There are two x-terms in the resulting expression, $4x$ and $-3x$. Combine them by adding their coefficients:

$$4x + 6y - 3x = 1x + 6y$$

$$= x + 6y$$

WORD PROBLEMS AND APPLICATIONS

1. C: The volume of the box is the product of $\sqrt{3}$, $2\sqrt{5}$, and 4. To multiply two or more square root radicals, multiply the coefficients and then multiply the radicands:

$$\sqrt{3} \times 2\sqrt{5} \times 4 = 2\sqrt{15} \times 4$$

$$= 8\sqrt{15}$$

2. D: The cost of the cab ride is $3.60 plus $0.75 times the distance, excluding the first half-mile. This is given by the expression $3.60 + 0.75(d - 0.5)$.

3. D: First create variables for the two unknowns in the problem. Let d represent the number of dimes and q represent the number of quarters. Given that Adam has 24 coins and that the coins are worth $3.30 altogether, a system of linear equations can be defined:

$$d + q = 24$$

$$10d + 24q = 330$$

Solve this system of equations using the elimination method. To eliminate q, multiply the first equation by 25, and then subtract the equations from one another:

$$25(d + q = 24) \qquad 25d + 25q = 600$$
$$10 + 25q = 330 \qquad -(10d + 25q = 330)$$

$$15d + 0 = 270$$

Finally, solve the resulting equation by dividing both sides by 15. The result is $d = 18$, which means that Adam has 18 dimes.

4. A: First establish a variable, s, for the length of the smaller square. Since the larger square is 3 feet longer than the smaller one, its length is $s + 3$. Given that the difference between the areas of the two squares is 75, and the area of any square is equal to its side lengths squared, the following equation can be established:

$$(s + 3)^2 - s^2 = 75$$

Simplify the left side of the equation:

$$(s + 3)^2 - s^2 = 75$$

$$(s + 3)(s + 3) - s^2 = 75$$

$$s^2 + 6s + 9 - s^2 = 75$$

$$6s + 9 = 75$$

Isolate the variable and divide both sides by its coefficient to solve for s:

$$6s = 66$$

$$s = 11$$

Therefore, the length of the smaller square is 11 feet.

5. C: The ball will hit the ground when its height is zero. In mathematical notation, this will happen when the expression for its height is equal to zero:

$$-16t^2 + 47t + 3 = 0$$

To solve this equation, factor the expression on the left side of the equation and then use the zero-product rule:

$$(-t + 3)(16t + 1) = 0$$

$$-t + 3 = 0 \quad \text{or} \quad 16t + 1 = 0$$

$$t = 3 \qquad\qquad t = -\frac{1}{16}$$

The answer only makes sense when t is positive, so discard the negative value. Thus, the ball will hit the ground exactly 3 seconds after it is thrown.

College Level Mathematics

ALGEBRAIC OPERATIONS

1. D: The given expression is a trinomial that can be factored. Since the expression is a trinomial of degree 4 (not 2), create a temporary variable, u, to put it in quadratic form and eventually factor it. Letting $u = y^2$, substitute u for every occurrence of y^2 in the given expression:

$$y^4 + 3y^2 - 4 = (y^2)^2 + 3(y^2) - 4$$

$$= u^2 + 3u - 4$$

Next, factor the resulting expression:

$$u^2 + 3u - 4 = (u + 4)(u - 1)$$

Since u was only a temporary variable created to make the problem easier, substitute y^2 back in the expression:

$$(u + 4)(u - 1) = (y^2 + 4)(y^2 - 1)$$

This is a valid factorization for the original expression. However, it can be factored further since $y^2 - 1$ is the difference of two squares:

$$(y^2 + 4)(y^2 - 1) = (y^2 + 4)(y - 1)(y + 1)$$

2. C: To simplify the expression, start by factoring the numerator and denominator. For the numerator, find two numbers whose sum is −3 and whose product is −10, and then put those numbers into the form $(x + a)(x + b)$. For the denominator, factor out the greatest common factor (GCF), which is 4:

$$\frac{x^2 - 3x - 10}{4x - 20} = \frac{(x-5)(x+2)}{4(x-5)}$$

Last, simplify the expression by cancelling out the common factor of $(x - 5)$:

$$\frac{(x-5)(x+2)}{4(x-5)} = \frac{x+2}{4}$$

3. D: First use the definition of an exponent to rewrite the given expression as the product of two trinomials:

$$(2n^2 + 3n + 1)^2 = (2n^2 + 3n + 1)(2n^2 + 3n + 1)$$

Next, multiply each term in the first trinomial by the second trinomial (in its entirety):

$$(2n^2 + 3n + 1)(2n^2 + 3n + 1) =$$

$$2n^2(2n^2 + 3n + 1) + 3n(2n^2 + 3n + 1) + 1(2n^2 + 3n + 1)$$

Finally, distribute the three products and combine like terms in the result:

$$2n^2(2n^2 + 3n + 1) + 3n(2n^2 + 3n + 1) + 1(2n^2 + 3n + 1)$$

$$= (4n^4 + 6n^3 + 2n^2) + (6n^3 + 9n^2 + 3n) + (2n^2 + 3n + 1)$$

$$= 4n^4 + 12n^3 + 13n^2 + 6n + 1$$

4. B: Raising a number or an expression to a negative power is the same thing as raising it to a positive power and then taking the reciprocal of the result. As a result, the given expression is equal to the reciprocal of $(4a)^2$:

$$(4a)^{-2} = \frac{1}{(4a)^2}$$

Simplify the denominator in this expression by distributing the now-positive exponent:

$$\frac{1}{(4a)^2} = \frac{1}{16a^2}$$

5. C: Exponential expressions can only be subtracted if they have the same base and exponent (and only differ in coefficients.) The given terms have the same base but not the same exponent. The difference between the exponents is $\frac{5}{2} - \frac{3}{2} = 1$. Therefore, taking out a 3 (thus reducing the exponent by 1) from the first term will make the remaining values like terms that can then be combined:

$$3^{\frac{5}{2}} - 3^{\frac{3}{2}} = 3 \cdot 3^{\frac{3}{2}} - 1 \cdot 3^{\frac{3}{2}}$$

$$= (3 - 1) \cdot 3^{\frac{3}{2}}$$

$$= 2 \cdot 3^{\frac{3}{2}}$$

The result can now be written as a radical expression with no exponents. Start by taking out another 3 from $3^{\frac{3}{2}}$:

$$2 \cdot 3^{\frac{3}{2}} = 2 \cdot 3 \cdot 3^{\frac{1}{2}}$$

$$= 6 \cdot 3^{\frac{1}{2}}$$

Last, use the rule $a^{\frac{m}{n}} = \left(\sqrt[n]{a}\right)^m = \sqrt[n]{a^m}$ to rewrite the exponent as a square root:

$$6 \cdot 3^{\frac{1}{2}} = 6\sqrt{3}$$

SOLUTIONS OF EQUATIONS AND INEQUALITIES

1. D: Start by rewriting the equation in the form $ax^2 + bx + c = 0$ by subtracting 1 from both sides:

$$4x^2 + 2x = 1$$

$$4x^2 + 2x - 1 = 0$$

The left side cannot be factored, so use the quadratic formula. For the variables in the quadratic formula, use $a = 4$, $b = 2$, and $c = -1$:

$$x = \frac{-b \pm \sqrt{b^2 - 4ac}}{2a}$$

$$= \frac{-(2) \pm \sqrt{(2)^2 - 4(4)(-1)}}{2(4)}$$

$$= \frac{-2 \pm \sqrt{4 + 16}}{8}$$

$$= \frac{-2 \pm \sqrt{20}}{8}$$

$$= \frac{-2 \pm 2\sqrt{5}}{8}$$

$$= -\frac{1}{4} \pm \frac{\sqrt{5}}{4}$$

2. B: Solve the inequality by changing the inequality sign to an equal sign and solve the resulting equation by factoring the left side:

$$x^2 - 7x + 10 = 0$$

$$(x - 2)(x - 5) = 0$$

$$x - 2 = 0 \quad \text{or} \quad x - 5 = 0$$

$$x = 2 \qquad\qquad x = 5$$

Since the original inequality sign was a greater-than-or-equal-to sign (rather than just a greater-than sign), the solution set will include $x = 2$ and $x = 5$.

These two solutions divide the number line into three distinct regions: $x < 2$, $2 < x < 5$, and $x > 5$. To see which regions are in the solution set, pick one test value from each region and substitute it in the original inequality. If the result is a true inequality, then the whole region is part of the solution set. Otherwise, the whole region is not part in the solution set:

Region	Test Value	$x^2 - 7x + 10 \geq 0$	Conclusion
$x < 2$	0	$(0)^2 - 7(0) + 10 \geq 0$ $10 \geq 0$	Part of the solution set
$2 < x < 5$	3	$(3)^2 - 7(3) + 10 \geq 0$ $9 - 21 + 10 \geq 0$ $-2 \geq 0$	Not part of the solution set
$x > 5$	6	$(6)^2 - 7(6) + 10 \geq 0$ $36 - 42 + 10 \geq 0$ $4 \geq 0$	Part of the solution set

Therefore, the solution set is $x \leq 2$ or $x \geq 5$.

3. A: The given equations form a system of three linear equation with three variables $x, y,$ and z. Organize the equations by writing them vertically with the corresponding variables lined up:

$$(1) \quad x + 2y \qquad\quad = 1$$
$$(2) \qquad\quad 3y + z = 1$$
$$(3) \; -x + y + 3z = 8$$

Now solve the system using the elimination method. Since equation (1) has an x and equation (2) has a $-x$, add them to eliminate x. The result is a new equation, equation (4), which only has y and z for variables:

$$\begin{array}{l} (1)\; x + 2y \qquad\quad = 1 \\ (3)\; \underline{-x + y + 3z = 8} \\ (4) \qquad\; 3y + 3z = 9 \end{array}$$

Next subtract equation (2) from equation (4) to eliminate y:

$$\begin{array}{l} (4) \qquad\; 3y + 3z = 9 \\ (2) \qquad \underline{-(3y + z) = -1} \\ (5) \qquad\qquad\;\; 2z = 8 \end{array}$$

If you solve the resulting equation for z, you get the value $z = 4$. Use this value to calculate the value of y since the value of x cannot be determined from z. Start by substituting 4 for z in equation (2) and solve for y:

$$(2)\, 3y + (4) = 1$$
$$3y = -3$$
$$y = -1$$

Finally, substitute −1 for *y* in equation (1) and solve the resulting equation for *x*.

$$(1) \quad x + 2y = 1$$

$$x + 2(-1) = 1$$

$$x = 3$$

4. D: To solve the equation, first get rid of the denominators by multiplying both sides of the equation by $x(x-3)$ and simplifying the result:

$$\frac{4}{x-3} - \frac{2}{x} = 1$$

$$x(x-3)\left[\frac{4}{x-3} - \frac{2}{x}\right] = x(x-3) \cdot 1$$

$$4x - 2(x-3) = x(x-3)$$

$$4x - 2x + 6 = x^2 - 3x$$

$$2x + 6 = x^2 - 3x$$

The result is a quadratic equation. Move everything to one side and then solve for *x* by factoring the left side and applying the zero-product rule:

$$x^2 - 5x - 6 = 0$$

$$(x + 1)(x - 6) = 0$$

$$x + 1 = 0 \quad \text{or} \quad x - 6 = 0$$

$$x = -1 \qquad\qquad x = 6$$

Therefore, the possible solutions are $x = -1$ and $x = 6$. Since neither of these values will cause division by zero when substituted back into the original equation, they are both valid solutions.

5. B: Start by squaring both sides of the equation and simplifying the result:

$$\left(\sqrt{3x - 2}\right)^2 = (x - 2)^2$$

$$3x - 2 = x^2 - 4x + 4$$

Next, move everything to one side and factor to find solutions for x:

$$x^2 - 7x + 6 = 0$$

$$(x - 1)(x - 6) = 0$$

$$x - 1 = 0 \quad \text{or} \quad x - 6 = 0$$

$$x = 1 \qquad\qquad x = 6$$

Therefore, the possible solutions are $x = 1$ and $x = 6$. Substitute these solutions into the original equation to see if they are valid solutions:

$$\sqrt{3x - 2} = x - 2$$
$$\sqrt{3(1) - 2} = (1) - 2$$
$$\sqrt{1} = 1 - 2$$
$$1 = 1 - 2 \text{ False}$$

$$\sqrt{3x - 2} = x - 2$$
$$\sqrt{3(6) - 2} = (6) - 2$$
$$\sqrt{16} = 6 - 2$$
$$4 = 6 - 2 \text{ True}$$

Since only $x = 6$ leads to a true equality, that is the only solution.

COORDINATE GEOMETRY

1. A: The coordinates of a point are an ordered pair (x, y) that indicate where the point is located on the coordinate plane. Find the coordinates by determining the distance each point is from both the x and y axes. The leftmost point is 1 unit to the left of the y-axis and sits on the x-axis. Therefore, its coordinates are $(-1, 0)$. The top point is 2 units to the right of the y-axis and 4 units above the x-axis, or $(2, 4)$. The bottom point is 2 units to the right of the y-axis and 2 units below the x-axis, of $(2, -2)$.

2. A: The equation of line L is given in slope-intercept form $y = mx + b$, therefore the slope of line L is $m = 3$, while its y-intercept is $b = 1$.

Two lines are perpendicular if their slopes are negative reciprocals. Since the slope of line L is 3, the slope of a line perpendicular to it must be $= -\frac{1}{3}$. Substitute this value into the general slope-intercept form $y = mx + b$ to find an equation for any perpendicular to L:

$$y = -\frac{1}{3}x + b$$

Since the point $(-3, -5)$ must be intersected by the perpendicular line, and is thus a point on that line, substitute $x = -3$ and $y = -5$ into the equation above and then solve for b:

$$(-5) = -\frac{1}{3}(-3) + b$$

$$-5 = 1 + b$$

$$-6 = b$$

Finally, plug this value for b into the equation $y = -\frac{1}{3}x + b$ to obtain the solution:

$$y = -\frac{1}{3}x - 6$$

3. A: A conic section is a curve obtained by the intersection of a cone and a plane. The four conic sections are the circle, the ellipse, the parabola, and the hyperbola. The following chart shows a general equation for each of the four conic sections:

Conic Section	Equation
Circle	$(x - h)^2 + (y - k)^2 = r^2$
Ellipse	$\dfrac{(x-h)^2}{a^2} + \dfrac{(y-k)^2}{b^2} = 1$
Parabola	$(x - h)^2 = 4a(y - k)$
Hyperbola	$\dfrac{(x-h)^2}{a^2} - \dfrac{(y-k)^2}{b^2} = 1$

The given equation can be rewritten as $(x - 0)^2 + (y - 0)^2 = (\sqrt{11})^2$, thus it is the equation of a circle.

4. B: The graph of a quadratic equation is a parabola, a U-shaped curve, which is also one of the four conic sections. To graph the given equation, substitute three or more values of x into the given equation and then calculate the corresponding values of y. The results are shown in the table of values below:

x	$y = x^2 + 2x - 1$	(x,y)
−2	$(-2)^2 + 2(-2) - 1 = -1$	(−2,−1)
−1	$(-1)^2 + 2(-1) - 1 = -2$	(−1,−2)
0	$(0)^2 + 2(0) - 1 = -1$	(0,−1)
1	$(1)^2 + 2(1) - 1 = 2$	(1,2)
2	$(2)^2 + 2(2) - 1 = 7$	(2,7)

From the table, the graph of the equation must pass through the points, (−2,−1), (−1,−2), (0,−1), (1,2), and (2,7). Graph these points on a coordinate plane and then connect them with a parabola line. This result matches graph B:

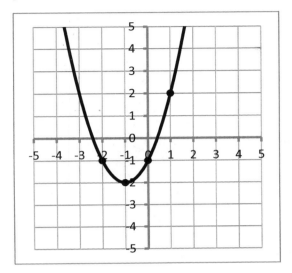

5. D: To graph an inequality, first graph its boundary line(s). Change the inequality sign to an equal sign and graph the resulting equation, $y = 3x + 1$. Since the given inequality is a less-than-or-equal-to sign graph it using a solid line (rather than a dotted one):

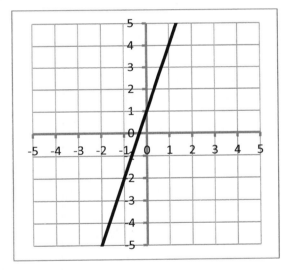

Next, to determine which region to shade, choose a test point in one of the regions. The easiest point to test is the origin (0, 0). Substitute $x = 0$ and $y = 0$ into the given inequality; if the result is a true inequality, then the whole region that contains the origin should be shaded, otherwise, the other region should be shaded:

$$y \leq 3x + 1$$

$$0 \leq 3(0) + 1$$

$$0 \leq 1$$

Since the result is a true inequality, shade the region to the right of the line:

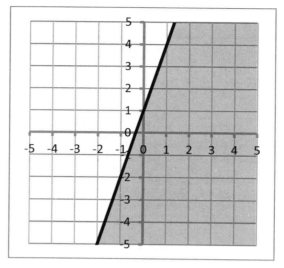

APPLICATIONS AND OTHER ALGEBRA TOPICS

1. C: Start by rewriting the equation in the form $ax^2 + bx + c = 0$. Distribute the left side and then move everything to one side:

$$2x(x + 1) = -3$$

$$2x^2 + 2x = -3$$

$$2x^2 + 2x + 3 = 0$$

Since the left side cannot be factored, use the quadratic formula to solve the equation. For the variables in the quadratic formula, use $a = 2$, $b = 2$, and $c = 3$:

$$x = \frac{-b \pm \sqrt{b^2 - 4ac}}{2a}$$

$$= \frac{-(2) \pm \sqrt{(2)^2 - 4(2)(3)}}{2(2)}$$

$$= \frac{-2 \pm \sqrt{-20}}{4}$$

The result contains the square root of a negative number, so the solution is not a real number. Instead, it is a complex number that contains the imaginary number i, which is the square root of -1:

$$x = \frac{-2 \pm \sqrt{-1} \times \sqrt{20}}{4}$$

$$= \frac{-2 \pm 2i\sqrt{5}}{4}$$

$$= -\frac{1}{2} \pm \frac{i\sqrt{5}}{2}$$

86

2. D: Each term in the sequence is 3 more than the last. Therefore, this sequence is an arithmetic sequence with a common difference d of 3.

To find the sum of the first 20 terms of the sequence, begin by calculating the first term, a_1, as well as the 20th term, a_{20}, of the given sequence. The first term is given in the problem. Its value is $a_1 = 2$. The 20th term, however, must be found by using the formula for the nth term of an arithmetic sequence:

$$a_n = a_1 + (n-1)d$$

Substitute the values $n = 20$, $a_1 = 2$, and $d = 3$ into this formula and then simplify the result:

$$a_{20} = 2 + (20-1) \cdot 3$$

$$= 2 + 19 \cdot 3$$

$$= 59$$

Therefore, the 20th term in the sequence is 59. Next solve the problem by using the formula for the sum of the first n terms of an arithmetic sequence:

$$S_n = \frac{n}{2}(a_1 + a_n)$$

Substitute the values $n = 20$, $a_1 = 2$, and $a_{20} = 59$ into the formula and then simplify the result:

$$S_{20} = \frac{20}{2}(2 + 59)$$

$$= 10 \cdot 61$$

$$= 610$$

3. D: The number of bacteria in the Petri dish doubles every day, so the first four days are:

Day	1	2	3	4
Number of Bacteria	500	1000	2000	4000

The number of bacteria forms a sequence in which each term is two times the last. Therefore, this sequence is a geometric sequence with a common ratio r of 2. Calculate the 14th term of the sequence using the formula for the nth term of the geometric term:

$$a_n = a_1 r^{n-1}$$

Substitute the values $n = 14$, $a_1 = 500$, and $r = 2$ into the formula and then simplify the result:

$$a_{14} = 500 \cdot 2^{14-1}$$

$$= 500 \cdot 2^{13}$$

$$= 500 \cdot 8{,}192$$

$$= 409{,}600$$

Therefore, the Petri dish will contain 409,600 bacteria after 14 days.

4. B: A permutation is an arrangement of a set of objects in which the order of the objects does matter. The notation $_nP_k$ gives the number of different permutation you can make if you use a total of n objects to form a group of k objects without using an object more than once. The value of $_nP_k$ can be found using the formula below:

$$_nP_k = \frac{n!}{(n-k)!}$$

In this problem, the committee is electing four people for four separate positions from a pool of 12 people. Thus, to find the number of possible outcomes, calculate $_{12}P_4$:

$$_{12}P_4 = \frac{12!}{(12-4)!}$$

$$= \frac{12 \times 11 \times \ldots \times 1}{8 \times 7 \times \ldots \times 1}$$

$$= \frac{12 \times 11 \times 10 \times 9}{1}$$

$$= 11,880$$

Therefore, there are 11,880 ways that the committee can elect the four positions.

5. A: A. combination is an arrangement of a set of objects in which the order of the objects does not matter. The notation $\binom{n}{k}$ gives the number of different combinations you can make if you use a total of n objects to form a group of k objects without using an object more than once. The value of $\binom{n}{k}$ can be found using the formula below:

$$\binom{n}{k} = \frac{n!}{k!(n-k)!}$$

This problem wants the total number of five-card hands that are only spades. Two hands that have the same five cards but are given in different orders (e.g. the 2, 3, 4, 5, 6 of spades and the 6, 5, 4, 3, 2 of spades) are considered the same hand. Therefore, the order of the five cards does not matter. Since there are only 13 spades in a standard deck, calculate the number of combinations of five cards that can be formed from the 13 spades. This value is given by $\binom{13}{5}$:

$$\binom{13}{5} = \frac{13!}{5!(13-5)!}$$

$$= \frac{13 \times 12 \times \ldots \times 1}{(5 \times 4 \times \ldots \times 1) \times (8 \times 7 \times \ldots \times 1)}$$

$$= \frac{13 \times 12 \times 11 \times 10 \times 9}{5 \times 4 \times 3 \times 2 \times 1}$$

$$= \frac{154,440}{120}$$

$$= 1287$$

Thus, there are 1287 different five-card hands that consist only of spades.

FUNCTIONS AND TRIGONOMETRY

1. C: Calculate $f\left(-\frac{1}{2}\right)$ by substituting $-\frac{1}{2}$ for x in $4x^3 + 5x^2 - 2$ and simplifying the result:

$$f\left(-\frac{1}{2}\right) = 4\left(-\frac{1}{2}\right)^3 + 5\left(-\frac{1}{2}\right)^2 - 2$$

$$= 4\left(-\frac{1}{8}\right) + 5\left(\frac{1}{4}\right) - 2$$

$$= -\frac{1}{2} + \frac{5}{4} - 2$$

$$= -\frac{5}{4}$$

2. A: The domain of a function is the set of all possible input values that can be evaluated by a function. The easiest way to find the domain of the given function g is to look at all the different operations that are used in the function to determine if one or more of them is not defined for some values of x. The domain will be the set of all real numbers, except those x-values.

Since $g(x)$ is a rational function with $x + 2$ in the denominator and division by zero is undefined, the domain of the function is all real numbers except $x = -2$, which is usually written as $x \neq -2$.

3. B: The composition of two functions is a function that is formed by combining the two functions so that the output of one of them is the input of the other. Find the composition by substituting the output of $g(x)$, $\frac{3x+1}{2}$, for the input of $f(x)$, x, and simplifying the result:

$$(f \circ g)(x) = f\left(\frac{3x+1}{2}\right)$$

$$= 2\left(\frac{3x + 1}{2}\right) - 4$$

$$= (3x + 1) - 4$$

$$= 3x - 3$$

4. C: The inverse of a function is a function that undoes the original function. To find $h^{-1}(x)$, start with the definition of $h(x)$ and then replace $h(x)$ with y:

$$h(x) = \log_{10}(x + 2)$$

$$y = \log_{10}(x + 2)$$

Then switch all of the x's and y's:

$$x = \log_{10}(y + 2)$$

Next solve the resulting equation for y. The logarithm of a number is the exponent that the base must to be raised to in order to get that number. Using this definition, rewrite the logarithmic equation as an exponential one and then solve for y:

$$y + 2 = 10^x$$

89

$$y = 10^x - 2$$

Finally, replace y with $h^{-1}(x)$:

$$h^{-1}(x) = 10^x - 2$$

5. D: Trigonometric functions are functions of an angle that are based on the proportions of a right triangle. Given that $\sin \theta = \frac{5}{7}$, and $sin = \frac{opposite}{hypotenuse}$, the side opposite θ is 5 units long and the hypotenuse is 7 units long. The remaining side length is an unknown, x.

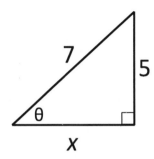

Calculate the missing side x using the Pythagorean Theorem:

$$a^2 + b^2 = c^2$$

$$x^2 + 5^2 = 7^2$$

$$x^2 + 25 = 49$$

$$x^2 = 24$$

$$x = 2\sqrt{6}$$

Finally, calculate the value of cos θ:

$$\cos \theta = \frac{adjacent}{hypotenuse}$$

$$= \frac{2\sqrt{6}}{7}$$

How to Overcome Test Anxiety

Just the thought of taking a test is enough to make most people a little nervous. A test is an important event that can have a long-term impact on your future, so it's important to take it seriously and it's natural to feel anxious about performing well. But just because anxiety is normal, that doesn't mean that it's helpful in test taking, or that you should simply accept it as part of your life. Anxiety can have a variety of effects. These effects can be mild, like making you feel slightly nervous, or severe, like blocking your ability to focus or remember even a simple detail.

If you experience test anxiety—whether severe or mild—it's important to know how to beat it. To discover this, first you need to understand what causes test anxiety.

Causes of Test Anxiety

While we often think of anxiety as an uncontrollable emotional state, it can actually be caused by simple, practical things. One of the most common causes of test anxiety is that a person does not feel adequately prepared for their test. This feeling can be the result of many different issues such as poor study habits or lack of organization, but the most common culprit is time management. Starting to study too late, failing to organize your study time to cover all of the material, or being distracted while you study will mean that you're not well prepared for the test. This may lead to cramming the night before, which will cause you to be physically and mentally exhausted for the test. Poor time management also contributes to feelings of stress, fear, and hopelessness as you realize you are not well prepared but don't know what to do about it.

Other times, test anxiety is not related to your preparation for the test but comes from unresolved fear. This may be a past failure on a test, or poor performance on tests in general. It may come from comparing yourself to others who seem to be performing better or from the stress of living up to expectations. Anxiety may be driven by fears of the future—how failure on this test would affect your educational and career goals. These fears are often completely irrational, but they can still negatively impact your test performance.

> **Review Video: <u>3 Reasons You Have Test Anxiety</u>**
> Visit mometrix.com/academy and enter code: 428468

Elements of Test Anxiety

As mentioned earlier, test anxiety is considered to be an emotional state, but it has physical and mental components as well. Sometimes you may not even realize that you are suffering from test anxiety until you notice the physical symptoms. These can include trembling hands, rapid heartbeat, sweating, nausea, and tense muscles. Extreme anxiety may lead to fainting or vomiting. Obviously, any of these symptoms can have a negative impact on testing. It is important to recognize them as soon as they begin to occur so that you can address the problem before it damages your performance.

Review Video: 3 Ways to Tell You Have Test Anxiety
Visit mometrix.com/academy and enter code: 927847

The mental components of test anxiety include trouble focusing and inability to remember learned information. During a test, your mind is on high alert, which can help you recall information and stay focused for an extended period of time. However, anxiety interferes with your mind's natural processes, causing you to blank out, even on the questions you know well. The strain of testing during anxiety makes it difficult to stay focused, especially on a test that may take several hours. Extreme anxiety can take a huge mental toll, making it difficult not only to recall test information but even to understand the test questions or pull your thoughts together.

Review Video: How Test Anxiety Affects Memory
Visit mometrix.com/academy and enter code: 609003

Effects of Test Anxiety

Test anxiety is like a disease—if left untreated, it will get progressively worse. Anxiety leads to poor performance, and this reinforces the feelings of fear and failure, which in turn lead to poor performances on subsequent tests. It can grow from a mild nervousness to a crippling condition. If allowed to progress, test anxiety can have a big impact on your schooling, and consequently on your future.

Test anxiety can spread to other parts of your life. Anxiety on tests can become anxiety in any stressful situation, and blanking on a test can turn into panicking in a job situation. But fortunately, you don't have to let anxiety rule your testing and determine your grades. There are a number of relatively simple steps you can take to move past anxiety and function normally on a test and in the rest of life.

Review Video: How Test Anxiety Impacts Your Grades
Visit mometrix.com/academy and enter code: 939819

Physical Steps for Beating Test Anxiety

While test anxiety is a serious problem, the good news is that it can be overcome. It doesn't have to control your ability to think and remember information. While it may take time, you can begin taking steps today to beat anxiety.

Just as your first hint that you may be struggling with anxiety comes from the physical symptoms, the first step to treating it is also physical. Rest is crucial for having a clear, strong mind. If you are tired, it is much easier to give in to anxiety. But if you establish good sleep habits, your body and mind will be ready to perform optimally, without the strain of exhaustion. Additionally, sleeping well helps you to retain information better, so you're more likely to recall the answers when you see the test questions.

Getting good sleep means more than going to bed on time. It's important to allow your brain time to relax. Take study breaks from time to time so it doesn't get overworked, and don't study right before bed. Take time to rest your mind before trying to rest your body, or you may find it difficult to fall asleep.

Review Video: The Importance of Sleep for Your Brain
Visit mometrix.com/academy and enter code: 319338

Along with sleep, other aspects of physical health are important in preparing for a test. Good nutrition is vital for good brain function. Sugary foods and drinks may give a burst of energy but this burst is followed by a crash, both physically and emotionally. Instead, fuel your body with protein and vitamin-rich foods.

Also, drink plenty of water. Dehydration can lead to headaches and exhaustion, especially if your brain is already under stress from the rigors of the test. Particularly if your test is a long one, drink water during the breaks. And if possible, take an energy-boosting snack to eat between sections.

Review Video: How Diet Can Affect your Mood
Visit mometrix.com/academy and enter code: 624317

Along with sleep and diet, a third important part of physical health is exercise. Maintaining a steady workout schedule is helpful, but even taking 5-minute study breaks to walk can help get your blood pumping faster and clear your head. Exercise also releases endorphins, which contribute to a positive feeling and can help combat test anxiety.

When you nurture your physical health, you are also contributing to your mental health. If your body is healthy, your mind is much more likely to be healthy as well. So take time to rest, nourish your body with healthy food and water, and get moving as much as possible. Taking these physical steps will make you stronger and more able to take the mental steps necessary to overcome test anxiety.

Review Video: How to Stay Healthy and Prevent Test Anxiety
Visit mometrix.com/academy and enter code: 877894

Mental Steps for Beating Test Anxiety

Working on the mental side of test anxiety can be more challenging, but as with the physical side, there are clear steps you can take to overcome it. As mentioned earlier, test anxiety often stems from lack of preparation, so the obvious solution is to prepare for the test. Effective studying may be the most important weapon you have for beating test anxiety, but you can and should employ several other mental tools to combat fear.

First, boost your confidence by reminding yourself of past success—tests or projects that you aced. If you're putting as much effort into preparing for this test as you did for those, there's no reason you should expect to fail here. Work hard to prepare; then trust your preparation.

Second, surround yourself with encouraging people. It can be helpful to find a study group, but be sure that the people you're around will encourage a positive attitude. If you spend time with others who are anxious or cynical, this will only contribute to your own anxiety. Look for others who are motivated to study hard from a desire to succeed, not from a fear of failure.

Third, reward yourself. A test is physically and mentally tiring, even without anxiety, and it can be helpful to have something to look forward to. Plan an activity following the test, regardless of the outcome, such as going to a movie or getting ice cream.

When you are taking the test, if you find yourself beginning to feel anxious, remind yourself that you know the material. Visualize successfully completing the test. Then take a few deep, relaxing breaths and return to it. Work through the questions carefully but with confidence, knowing that you are capable of succeeding.

Developing a healthy mental approach to test taking will also aid in other areas of life. Test anxiety affects more than just the actual test—it can be damaging to your mental health and even contribute to depression. It's important to beat test anxiety before it becomes a problem for more than testing.

Review Video: <u>Test Anxiety and Depression</u>
Visit mometrix.com/academy and enter code: 904704

Study Strategy

Being prepared for the test is necessary to combat anxiety, but what does being prepared look like? You may study for hours on end and still not feel prepared. What you need is a strategy for test prep. The next few pages outline our recommended steps to help you plan out and conquer the challenge of preparation.

STEP 1: SCOPE OUT THE TEST

Learn everything you can about the format (multiple choice, essay, etc.) and what will be on the test. Gather any study materials, course outlines, or sample exams that may be available. Not only will this help you to prepare, but knowing what to expect can help to alleviate test anxiety.

STEP 2: MAP OUT THE MATERIAL

Look through the textbook or study guide and make note of how many chapters or sections it has. Then divide these over the time you have. For example, if a book has 15 chapters and you have five days to study, you need to cover three chapters each day. Even better, if you have the time, leave an extra day at the end for overall review after you have gone through the material in depth.

If time is limited, you may need to prioritize the material. Look through it and make note of which sections you think you already have a good grasp on, and which need review. While you are studying, skim quickly through the familiar sections and take more time on the challenging parts. Write out your plan so you don't get lost as you go. Having a written plan also helps you feel more in control of the study, so anxiety is less likely to arise from feeling overwhelmed at the amount to cover.

STEP 3: GATHER YOUR TOOLS

Decide what study method works best for you. Do you prefer to highlight in the book as you study and then go back over the highlighted portions? Or do you type out notes of the important information? Or is it helpful to make flashcards that you can carry with you? Assemble the pens, index cards, highlighters, post-it notes, and any other materials you may need so you won't be distracted by getting up to find things while you study.

If you're having a hard time retaining the information or organizing your notes, experiment with different methods. For example, try color-coding by subject with colored pens, highlighters, or post-it notes. If you learn better by hearing, try recording yourself reading your notes so you can listen while in the car, working out, or simply sitting at your desk. Ask a friend to quiz you from your flashcards, or try teaching someone the material to solidify it in your mind.

STEP 4: CREATE YOUR ENVIRONMENT

It's important to avoid distractions while you study. This includes both the obvious distractions like visitors and the subtle distractions like an uncomfortable chair (or a too-comfortable couch that makes you want to fall asleep). Set up the best study environment possible: good lighting and a comfortable work area. If background music helps you focus, you may want to turn it on, but otherwise keep the room quiet. If you are using a computer to take notes, be sure you don't have any other windows open, especially applications like social media, games, or anything else that could distract you. Silence your phone and turn off notifications. Be sure to keep water close by so you stay hydrated while you study (but avoid unhealthy drinks and snacks).

Also, take into account the best time of day to study. Are you freshest first thing in the morning? Try to set aside some time then to work through the material. Is your mind clearer in the afternoon or evening? Schedule your study session then. Another method is to study at the same time of day that

95

you will take the test, so that your brain gets used to working on the material at that time and will be ready to focus at test time.

STEP 5: STUDY!

Once you have done all the study preparation, it's time to settle into the actual studying. Sit down, take a few moments to settle your mind so you can focus, and begin to follow your study plan. Don't give in to distractions or let yourself procrastinate. This is your time to prepare so you'll be ready to fearlessly approach the test. Make the most of the time and stay focused.

Of course, you don't want to burn out. If you study too long you may find that you're not retaining the information very well. Take regular study breaks. For example, taking five minutes out of every hour to walk briskly, breathing deeply and swinging your arms, can help your mind stay fresh.

As you get to the end of each chapter or section, it's a good idea to do a quick review. Remind yourself of what you learned and work on any difficult parts. When you feel that you've mastered the material, move on to the next part. At the end of your study session, briefly skim through your notes again.

But while review is helpful, cramming last minute is NOT. If at all possible, work ahead so that you won't need to fit all your study into the last day. Cramming overloads your brain with more information than it can process and retain, and your tired mind may struggle to recall even previously learned information when it is overwhelmed with last-minute study. Also, the urgent nature of cramming and the stress placed on your brain contribute to anxiety. You'll be more likely to go to the test feeling unprepared and having trouble thinking clearly.

So don't cram, and don't stay up late before the test, even just to review your notes at a leisurely pace. Your brain needs rest more than it needs to go over the information again. In fact, plan to finish your studies by noon or early afternoon the day before the test. Give your brain the rest of the day to relax or focus on other things, and get a good night's sleep. Then you will be fresh for the test and better able to recall what you've studied.

STEP 6: TAKE A PRACTICE TEST

Many courses offer sample tests, either online or in the study materials. This is an excellent resource to check whether you have mastered the material, as well as to prepare for the test format and environment.

Check the test format ahead of time: the number of questions, the type (multiple choice, free response, etc.), and the time limit. Then create a plan for working through them. For example, if you have 30 minutes to take a 60-question test, your limit is 30 seconds per question. Spend less time on the questions you know well so that you can take more time on the difficult ones.

If you have time to take several practice tests, take the first one open book, with no time limit. Work through the questions at your own pace and make sure you fully understand them. Gradually work up to taking a test under test conditions: sit at a desk with all study materials put away and set a timer. Pace yourself to make sure you finish the test with time to spare and go back to check your answers if you have time.

After each test, check your answers. On the questions you missed, be sure you understand why you missed them. Did you misread the question (tests can use tricky wording)? Did you forget the information? Or was it something you hadn't learned? Go back and study any shaky areas that the practice tests reveal.

Taking these tests not only helps with your grade, but also aids in combating test anxiety. If you're already used to the test conditions, you're less likely to worry about it, and working through tests until you're scoring well gives you a confidence boost. Go through the practice tests until you feel comfortable, and then you can go into the test knowing that you're ready for it.

Test Tips

On test day, you should be confident, knowing that you've prepared well and are ready to answer the questions. But aside from preparation, there are several test day strategies you can employ to maximize your performance.

First, as stated before, get a good night's sleep the night before the test (and for several nights before that, if possible). Go into the test with a fresh, alert mind rather than staying up late to study.

Try not to change too much about your normal routine on the day of the test. It's important to eat a nutritious breakfast, but if you normally don't eat breakfast at all, consider eating just a protein bar. If you're a coffee drinker, go ahead and have your normal coffee. Just make sure you time it so that the caffeine doesn't wear off right in the middle of your test. Avoid sugary beverages, and drink enough water to stay hydrated but not so much that you need a restroom break 10 minutes into the test. If your test isn't first thing in the morning, consider going for a walk or doing a light workout before the test to get your blood flowing.

Allow yourself enough time to get ready, and leave for the test with plenty of time to spare so you won't have the anxiety of scrambling to arrive in time. Another reason to be early is to select a good seat. It's helpful to sit away from doors and windows, which can be distracting. Find a good seat, get out your supplies, and settle your mind before the test begins.

When the test begins, start by going over the instructions carefully, even if you already know what to expect. Make sure you avoid any careless mistakes by following the directions.

Then begin working through the questions, pacing yourself as you've practiced. If you're not sure on an answer, don't spend too much time on it, and don't let it shake your confidence. Either skip it and come back later, or eliminate as many wrong answers as possible and guess among the remaining ones. Don't dwell on these questions as you continue—put them out of your mind and focus on what lies ahead.

Be sure to read all of the answer choices, even if you're sure the first one is the right answer. Sometimes you'll find a better one if you keep reading. But don't second-guess yourself if you do immediately know the answer. Your gut instinct is usually right. Don't let test anxiety rob you of the information you know.

If you have time at the end of the test (and if the test format allows), go back and review your answers. Be cautious about changing any, since your first instinct tends to be correct, but make sure you didn't misread any of the questions or accidentally mark the wrong answer choice. Look over any you skipped and make an educated guess.

At the end, leave the test feeling confident. You've done your best, so don't waste time worrying about your performance or wishing you could change anything. Instead, celebrate the successful

completion of this test. And finally, use this test to learn how to deal with anxiety even better next time.

Review Video: 5 Tips to Beat Test Anxiety
Visit mometrix.com/academy and enter code: 570656

Important Qualification

Not all anxiety is created equal. If your test anxiety is causing major issues in your life beyond the classroom or testing center, or if you are experiencing troubling physical symptoms related to your anxiety, it may be a sign of a serious physiological or psychological condition. If this sounds like your situation, we strongly encourage you to seek professional help.

How to Overcome Your Fear of Math

The word *math* is enough to strike fear into most hearts. How many of us have memories of sitting through confusing lectures, wrestling over mind-numbing homework, or taking tests that still seem incomprehensible even after hours of study? Years after graduation, many still shudder at these memories.

The fact is, math is not just a classroom subject. It has real-world implications that you face every day, whether you realize it or not. This may be balancing your monthly budget, deciding how many supplies to buy for a project, or simply splitting a meal check with friends. The idea of daily confrontations with math can be so paralyzing that some develop a condition known as *math anxiety*.

But you do NOT need to be paralyzed by this anxiety! In fact, while you may have thought all your life that you're not good at math, or that your brain isn't wired to understand it, the truth is that you may have been conditioned to think this way. From your earliest school days, the way you were taught affected the way you viewed different subjects. And the way math has been taught has changed.

Several decades ago, there was a shift in American math classrooms. The focus changed from traditional problem-solving to a conceptual view of topics, de-emphasizing the importance of learning the basics and building on them. The solid foundation necessary for math progression and confidence was undermined. Math became more of a vague concept than a concrete idea. Today, it is common to think of math, not as a straightforward system, but as a mysterious, complicated method that can't be fully understood unless you're a genius.

This is why you may still have nightmares about being called on to answer a difficult problem in front of the class. Math anxiety is a very real, though unnecessary, fear.

Math anxiety may begin with a single class period. Let's say you missed a day in 6th grade math and never quite understood the concept that was taught while you were gone. Since math is cumulative, with each new concept building on past ones, this could very well affect the rest of your math career. Without that one day's knowledge, it will be difficult to understand any other concepts that link to it. Rather than realizing that you're just missing one key piece, you may begin to believe that you're simply not capable of understanding math.

This belief can change the way you approach other classes, career options, and everyday life experiences, if you become anxious at the thought that math might be required. A student who loves science may choose a different path of study upon realizing that multiple math classes will be required for a degree. An aspiring medical student may hesitate at the thought of going through the necessary math classes. For some this anxiety escalates into a more extreme state known as *math phobia*.

Math anxiety is challenging to address because it is rooted deeply and may come from a variety of causes: an embarrassing moment in class, a teacher who did not explain concepts well and contributed to a shaky foundation, or a failed test that contributed to the belief of math failure.

These causes add up over time, encouraged by society's popular view that math is hard and unpleasant. Eventually a person comes to firmly believe that he or she is simply bad at math. This belief makes it difficult to grasp new concepts or even remember old ones. Homework and test grades begin to slip, which only confirms the belief. The poor performance is not due to lack of ability but is caused by math anxiety.

Math anxiety is an emotional issue, not a lack of intelligence. But when it becomes deeply rooted, it can become more than just an emotional problem. Physical symptoms appear. Blood pressure may rise and heartbeat may quicken at the sight of a math problem – or even the thought of math! This fear leads to a mental block. When someone with math anxiety is asked to perform a calculation, even a basic problem can seem overwhelming and impossible. The emotional and physical response to the thought of math prevents the brain from working through it logically.

The more this happens, the more a person's confidence drops, and the more math anxiety is generated. This vicious cycle must be broken!

The first step in breaking the cycle is to go back to very beginning and make sure you really understand the basics of how math works and why it works. It is not enough to memorize rules for multiplication and division. If you don't know WHY these rules work, your foundation will be shaky and you will be at risk of developing a phobia. Understanding mathematical concepts not only promotes confidence and security, but allows you to build on this understanding for new concepts. Additionally, you can solve unfamiliar problems using familiar concepts and processes.

Why is it that students in other countries regularly outperform American students in math? The answer likely boils down to a couple of things: the foundation of mathematical conceptual understanding and societal perception. While students in the US are not expected to *like* or *get* math, in many other nations, students are expected not only to understand math but also to excel at it.

Changing the American view of math that leads to math anxiety is a monumental task. It requires changing the training of teachers nationwide, from kindergarten through high school, so that they learn to teach the *why* behind math and to combat the wrong math views that students may develop. It also involves changing the stigma associated with math, so that it is no longer viewed as unpleasant and incomprehensible. While these are necessary changes, they are challenging and will take time. But in the meantime, math anxiety is not irreversible—it can be faced and defeated, one person at a time.

False Beliefs

One reason math anxiety has taken such hold is that several false beliefs have been created and shared until they became widely accepted. Some of these unhelpful beliefs include the following:

There is only one way to solve a math problem. In the same way that you can choose from different driving routes and still arrive at the same house, you can solve a math problem using different methods and still find the correct answer. A person who understands the reasoning behind math calculations may be able to look at an unfamiliar concept and find the right answer, just by applying logic to the knowledge they already have. This approach may be different than what is taught in the classroom, but it is still valid. Unfortunately, even many teachers view math as a subject where the best course of action is to memorize the rule or process for each problem rather than as a place for students to exercise logic and creativity in finding a solution.

Many people don't have a mind for math. A person who has struggled due to poor teaching or math anxiety may falsely believe that he or she doesn't have the mental capacity to grasp mathematical concepts. Most of the time, this is false. Many people find that when they are relieved of their math anxiety, they have more than enough brainpower to understand math.

Men are naturally better at math than women. Even though research has shown this to be false, many young women still avoid math careers and classes because of their belief that their math abilities are inferior. Many girls have come to believe that math is a male skill and have given up trying to understand or enjoy it.

Counting aids are bad. Something like counting on your fingers or drawing out a problem to visualize it may be frowned on as childish or a crutch, but these devices can help you get a tangible understanding of a problem or a concept.

Sadly, many students buy into these ideologies at an early age. A young girl who enjoys math class may be conditioned to think that she doesn't actually have the brain for it because math is for boys, and may turn her energies to other pursuits, permanently closing the door on a wide range of opportunities. A child who finds the right answer but doesn't follow the teacher's method may believe that he is doing it wrong and isn't good at math. A student who never had a problem with math before may have a poor teacher and become confused, yet believe that the problem is because she doesn't have a mathematical mind.

Students who have bought into these erroneous beliefs quickly begin to add their own anxieties, adapting them to their own personal situations:

I'll never use this in real life. A huge number of people wrongly believe that math is irrelevant outside the classroom. By adopting this mindset, they are handicapping themselves for a life in a mathematical world, as well as limiting their career choices. When they are inevitably faced with real-world math, they are conditioning themselves to respond with anxiety.

I'm not quick enough. While timed tests and quizzes, or even simply comparing yourself with other students in the class, can lead to this belief, speed is not an indicator of skill level. A person can work very slowly yet understand at a deep level.

If I can understand it, it's too easy. People with a low view of their own abilities tend to think that if they are able to grasp a concept, it must be simple. They cannot accept the idea that they are capable of understanding math. This belief will make it harder to learn, no matter how intelligent they are.

I just can't learn this. An overwhelming number of people think this, from young children to adults, and much of the time it is simply not true. But this mindset can turn into a self-fulfilling prophecy that keeps you from exercising and growing your math ability.

The good news is, each of these myths can be debunked. For most people, they are based on emotion and psychology, NOT on actual ability! It will take time, effort, and the desire to change, but change is possible. Even if you have spent years thinking that you don't have the capability to understand math, it is not too late to uncover your true ability and find relief from the anxiety that surrounds math.

Math Strategies

It is important to have a plan of attack to combat math anxiety. There are many useful strategies for pinpointing the fears or myths and eradicating them:

Go back to the basics. For most people, math anxiety stems from a poor foundation. You may think that you have a complete understanding of addition and subtraction, or even decimals and percentages, but make absolutely sure. Learning math is different from learning other subjects. For example, when you learn history, you study various time periods and places and events. It may be important to memorize dates or find out about the lives of famous people. When you move from US history to world history, there will be some overlap, but a large amount of the information will be new. Mathematical concepts, on the other hand, are very closely linked and highly dependent on each other. It's like climbing a ladder – if a rung is missing from your understanding, it may be difficult or impossible for you to climb any higher, no matter how hard you try. So go back and make sure your math foundation is strong. This may mean taking a remedial math course, going to a tutor to work through the shaky concepts, or just going through your old homework to make sure you really understand it.

Speak the language. Math has a large vocabulary of terms and phrases unique to working problems. Sometimes these are completely new terms, and sometimes they are common words, but are used differently in a math setting. If you can't speak the language, it will be very difficult to get a thorough understanding of the concepts. It's common for students to think that they don't understand math when they simply don't understand the vocabulary. The good news is that this is fairly easy to fix. Brushing up on any terms you aren't quite sure of can help bring the rest of the concepts into focus.

Check your anxiety level. When you think about math, do you feel nervous or uncomfortable? Do you struggle with feelings of inadequacy, even on concepts that you know you've already learned? It's important to understand your specific math anxieties, and what triggers them. When you catch yourself falling back on a false belief, mentally replace it with the truth. Don't let yourself believe that you can't learn, or that struggling with a concept means you'll never understand it. Instead, remind yourself of how much you've already learned and dwell on that past success. Visualize grasping the new concept, linking it to your old knowledge, and moving on to the next challenge. Also, learn how to manage anxiety when it arises. There are many techniques for coping with the irrational fears that rise to the surface when you enter the math classroom. This may include controlled breathing, replacing negative thoughts with positive ones, or visualizing success. Anxiety interferes with your ability to concentrate and absorb information, which in turn contributes to greater anxiety. If you can learn how to regain control of your thinking, you will be better able to pay attention, make progress, and succeed!

Don't go it alone. Like any deeply ingrained belief, math anxiety is not easy to eradicate. And there is no need for you to wrestle through it on your own. It will take time, and many people find that speaking with a counselor or psychiatrist helps. They can help you develop strategies for responding to anxiety and overcoming old ideas. Additionally, it can be very helpful to take a short course or seek out a math tutor to help you find and fix the missing rungs on your ladder and make sure that you're ready to progress to the next level. You can also find a number of math aids online: courses that will teach you mental devices for figuring out problems, how to get the most out of your math classes, etc.

Check your math attitude. No matter how much you want to learn and overcome your anxiety, you'll have trouble if you still have a negative attitude toward math. If you think it's too hard, or just have general feelings of dread about math, it will be hard to learn and to break through the anxiety. Work on cultivating a positive math attitude. Remind yourself that math is not just a hurdle to be cleared, but a valuable asset. When you view math with a positive attitude, you'll be much more likely to understand and even enjoy it. This is something you must do for yourself. You may find it helpful to visit with a counselor. Your tutor, friends, and family may cheer you on in your endeavors. But your greatest asset is yourself. You are inside your own mind – tell yourself what you need to hear. Relive past victories. Remind yourself that you are capable of understanding math. Root out any false beliefs that linger and replace them with positive truths. Even if it doesn't feel true at first, it will begin to affect your thinking and pave the way for a positive, anxiety-free mindset.

Aside from these general strategies, there are a number of specific practical things you can do to begin your journey toward overcoming math anxiety. Something as simple as learning a new note-taking strategy can change the way you approach math and give you more confidence and understanding. New study techniques can also make a huge difference.

Math anxiety leads to bad habits. If it causes you to be afraid of answering a question in class, you may gravitate toward the back row. You may be embarrassed to ask for help. And you may procrastinate on assignments, which leads to rushing through them at the last moment when it's too late to get a better understanding. It's important to identify your negative behaviors and replace them with positive ones:

Prepare ahead of time. Read the lesson before you go to class. Being exposed to the topics that will be covered in class ahead of time, even if you don't understand them perfectly, is extremely helpful in increasing what you retain from the lecture. Do your homework and, if you're still shaky, go over some extra problems. The key to a solid understanding of math is practice.

Sit front and center. When you can easily see and hear, you'll understand more, and you'll avoid the distractions of other students if no one is in front of you. Plus, you're more likely to be sitting with students who are positive and engaged, rather than others with math anxiety. Let their positive math attitude rub off on you.

Ask questions in class and out. If you don't understand something, just ask. If you need a more in-depth explanation, the teacher may need to work with you outside of class, but often it's a simple concept you don't quite understand, and a single question may clear it up. If you wait, you may not be able to follow the rest of the day's lesson. For extra help, most professors have office hours outside of class when you can go over concepts one-on-one to clear up any uncertainties. Additionally, there may be a *math lab* or study session you can attend for homework help. Take advantage of this.

Review. Even if you feel that you've fully mastered a concept, review it periodically to reinforce it. Going over an old lesson has several benefits: solidifying your understanding, giving you a confidence boost, and even giving some new insights into material that you're currently learning! Don't let yourself get rusty. That can lead to problems with learning later concepts.

Teaching Tips

While the math student's mindset is the most crucial to overcoming math anxiety, it is also important for others to adjust their math attitudes. Teachers and parents have an enormous influence on how students relate to math. They can either contribute to math confidence or math anxiety.

As a parent or teacher, it is very important to convey a positive math attitude. Retelling horror stories of your own bad experience with math will contribute to a new generation of math anxiety. Even if you don't share your experiences, others will be able to sense your fears and may begin to believe them.

Even a careless comment can have a big impact, so watch for phrases like *He's not good at math* or *I never liked math.* You are a crucial role model, and your children or students will unconsciously adopt your mindset. Give them a positive example to follow. Rather than teaching them to fear the math world before they even know it, teach them about all its potential and excitement.

Work to present math as an integral, beautiful, and understandable part of life. Encourage creativity in solving problems. Watch for false beliefs and dispel them. Cross the lines between subjects: integrate history, English, and music with math. Show students how math is used every day, and how the entire world is based on mathematical principles, from the pull of gravity to the shape of seashells. Instead of letting students see math as a necessary evil, direct them to view it as an imaginative, beautiful art form – an art form that they are capable of mastering and using.

Don't give too narrow a view of math. It is more than just numbers. Yes, working problems and learning formulas is a large part of classroom math. But don't let the teaching stop there. Teach students about the everyday implications of math. Show them how nature works according to the laws of mathematics, and take them outside to make discoveries of their own. Expose them to math-related careers by inviting visiting speakers, asking students to do research and presentations, and learning students' interests and aptitudes on a personal level.

Demonstrate the importance of math. Many people see math as nothing more than a required stepping stone to their degree, a nuisance with no real usefulness. Teach students that algebra is used every day in managing their bank accounts, in following recipes, and in scheduling the day's events. Show them how learning to do geometric proofs helps them to develop logical thinking, an invaluable life skill. Let them see that math surrounds them and is integrally linked to their daily lives: that weather predictions are based on math, that math was used to design cars and other machines, etc. Most of all, give them the tools to use math to enrich their lives.

Make math as tangible as possible. Use visual aids and objects that can be touched. It is much easier to grasp a concept when you can hold it in your hands and manipulate it, rather than just listening to the lecture. Encourage math outside of the classroom. The real world is full of measuring, counting, and calculating, so let students participate in this. Keep your eyes open for numbers and patterns to discuss. Talk about how scores are calculated in sports games and how far apart plants are placed in a garden row for maximum growth. Build the mindset that math is a normal and interesting part of daily life.

Finally, find math resources that help to build a positive math attitude. There are a number of books that show math as fascinating and exciting while teaching important concepts, for example: *The Math Curse; A Wrinkle in Time; The Phantom Tollbooth;* and *Fractals, Googols and Other Mathematical Tales.* You can also find a number of online resources: math puzzles and games, videos that show math in nature, and communities of math enthusiasts. On a local level, students can compete in a variety of math competitions with other schools or join a math club.

The student who experiences math as exciting and interesting is unlikely to suffer from math anxiety. Going through life without this handicap is an immense advantage and opens many doors that others have closed through their fear.

Self-Check

Whether you suffer from math anxiety or not, chances are that you have been exposed to some of the false beliefs mentioned above. Now is the time to check yourself for any errors you may have accepted. Do you think you're not wired for math? Or that you don't need to understand it since you're not planning on a math career? Do you think math is just too difficult for the average person?

Find the errors you've taken to heart and replace them with positive thinking. Are you capable of learning math? Yes! Can you control your anxiety? Yes! These errors will resurface from time to time, so be watchful. Don't let others with math anxiety influence you or sway your confidence. If you're having trouble with a concept, find help. Don't let it discourage you!

Create a plan of attack for defeating math anxiety and sharpening your skills. Do some research and decide if it would help you to take a class, get a tutor, or find some online resources to fine-tune your knowledge. Make the effort to get good nutrition, hydration, and sleep so that you are operating at full capacity. Remind yourself daily that you are skilled and that anxiety does not control you. Your mind is capable of so much more than you know. Give it the tools it needs to grow and thrive.

Thank You

We at Mometrix would like to extend our heartfelt thanks to you, our friend and patron, for allowing us to play a part in your journey. It is a privilege to serve people from all walks of life who are unified in their commitment to building the best future they can for themselves.

The preparation you devote to these important testing milestones may be the most valuable educational opportunity you have for making a real difference in your life. We encourage you to put your heart into it—that feeling of succeeding, overcoming, and yes, conquering will be well worth the hours you've invested.

We want to hear your story, your struggles and your successes, and if you see any opportunities for us to improve our materials so we can help others even more effectively in the future, please share that with us as well. **The team at Mometrix would be absolutely thrilled to hear from you!** So please, send us an email (support@mometrix.com) and let's stay in touch.